TEN STEPS
TO RADICAL
SELF-CARE

TEN STEPS
TO RADICAL
SELF-CARE

Molly Kurland

Library of Congress Control Number: 2024909014
ISBN: Softcover   979-8-3694-1846-8
                   eBook   979-8-3694-1847-5

Rev. date: 06/05/2024

To order additional copies of this book, contact:
Xlibris
844-714-8691
www.Xlibris.com
Orders@Xlibris.com
858632

ACKNOWLEDGEMENTS

There are many people for whom I am grateful, who contributed to my personal growth and development, through their writings, workshops, classes and friendships. I was always a curious person, wanting to learn how to have an interesting life and how the things I was interested in worked. Since this book is about the various practices and routines I developed to strengthen and enhance my life, I want to give credit to those people who gave me the self-reliance to do things and try things, whether they were commonly done or not.

The first person who comes to mind is **Gordon Tappan**, who taught the first class I took at Sonoma State University. The class was Myths, Dreams and Symbols, about the work of psychologist Carl Jung and the way he explored human consciousness and how we, as individuals fit into a massive and diverse world.

Having always been a lover of movement and dance, I felt like I had found my place in the world when I discovered **Gabriel Roth**, who used dance and movement as a form of therapeutic evolution. Her books, "Sweat Your Prayers" and "Maps To Ecstasy" were like my holy bibles. I was fortunate to take a weeklong retreat with her, where we delved deeply into expressing our most genuine selves, mostly through movement but also through deeply honest verbal communication.

I was also lucky that **Ram Dass**, aka Richard Alpert, a spiritual teacher, who created his own movement, lived near me. He frequently had events nearby that I went to, including one he did for free for people in the healing arts professions. I received a personal invitation to his lecture, sent to my massage office. He said he was reaching out to local healers because this work is so important. He talked to us about helping people be as authentic as possible.

Paul Hawken rose to fame with his initial book, "The Magic of Findhorn" in 1975. In the 1980s, when I created my private practice in massage and hypnosis, I read his book, "Growing a Business", and that was the first book that began my exploration into the world of business and money and how to operate both successfully and with integrity. It rocked my world when one day, out of the blue, he came to my spa for a massage.

The author **Anne Lamott**, who inspired the title of this book, lives about an hour away from me. I have followed her since her first book, "Hard Laughter", came out in 1980, having attended more readings and events of hers than I can count. I love her humor, her honesty and her own creative ways of navigating life's difficulties. I became a fan of hers before she became wildly successful, back when she was mostly known through appearances on a local radio show and through readings at local bookstores.

Elizabeth Gilbert is another author who inspired me with honesty and authenticity. I've read all of her books since "Eat, Pray, Love" came out. Her book about creativity, "Big Magic" had a profound effect on me as a writer. It is one of my top favorites on creativity because it gives one permission to just be experimental and not worry about what comes of it. She said many things that I needed to hear. I've read it and listened to it repeatedly.

Shirley Merrifield greatly contributed to my development as a businesswoman, when I had my solo massage practice and expanded it into a day spa. She created an organization called Women in Business, which helped local women make connections, network, and grow their businesses through helping and learning from each other. She became my massage client and eventually a personal friend.

I was lucky to be part of the community of friends that included the writer, spiritual teacher and workshop leader, **Anodea Judith**, who founded Sacred Centers and taught us how to work with the seven chakras that make up significant parts of ourselves. She inspired me in so many ways.

I first encountered author and teacher, **Jacob Nordby** through his Facebook Page, Blessed Are The Weird, which resonated with me, because I immediately saw that he understood the connection between being unique and creativity. I took online classes from him and eventually attended his writing retreat, Heal and Create, which helped jump start me to get this book finalized. It was exciting to finally meet him in person at the retreat.

I also have to give credit to **Randal Churchill**, director of the Hypnotherapy Training Institute. He taught us how early experiences shape our emotional responses and therefore our behaviors and how to change adverse reactions through regression hypnotherapy. His classes were extremely powerful experiences which helped me grow as a person and be a better healer with my clients.

I was very blessed to connect with **Inga Aksamit** and **Norma Smith Davis**, who became my critique partners, as we were all writing non-fiction books. They were there when I wrote the first chapters of this book and gave me great, detailed notes that kept me writing.

The reader feedback from **Carla Hills**, **Ginny Matheson**, **Diane Darling**, and **Tracie Jansen** was enormously helpful when I shared the first draft of this book with them.

These people helped give me the confidence to be my own unique self and explore a creative way of navigating through life. Whenever I was dealing with difficult emotions, trying to figure out how to solve specific problems, or have a good time in unusual ways I thought about what I'd learned from them. I often had one of them sitting on my shoulder and whispering in my ear. For all of them I am deeply appreciative that our paths crossed when they did.

CONTENTS

CHAPTER 1

What Is Radical Self-Care?

What comes to mind when you think of self-care? Taking a hot bath? Getting a massage? Going away for a few days? What keeps you from taking care of yourself? Not having enough time? Getting distracted by too many other things that need your attention?

The word *radical* means "extreme." During one of her talks, I heard the author Anne Lamott use the term "radical self-care." It struck a chord with me because it emphasized it's something we need and often don't get, unless we make a powerful effort to do it ourselves. Often, the people who need it the most are the ones who are taking care of everyone else and leave themselves until last, and by that time, they are extremely desperate. Particularly if you are in a profession or play a role in your life where you are taking care of others, it can be wrenching to stop giving, step back, take a breath, and figure out what you need in order to recharge. The next step is figuring out how to change your routine to make time for yourself. It is easy to get burned out when you are continually putting energy into others and postponing taking care of yourself.

How Do We Change This?

Change is not easy. We are creatures of habit, so creating new routines takes a lot of effort until they become new habits. If you come home from work and focus on taking care of things in the house, whether it's getting dinner ready, checking in with your children or partner, dealing with all the messes leftover from yesterday, and then finally collapse in front of the TV, you're being consumed by your life. You may see an ad for a trip to the Caribbean that sounds really nice, but you know it's not going to happen. Instead, you think maybe you'll do something nice on the weekend. But then the weekend comes, and you wonder if you'll have time to relax after you finish all your chores. And before you know it, it's Sunday night, and you never really did anything special for yourself. But, definitely, you will do something next weekend. Definitely.

It's going to take a conscious effort to make solid changes. You have to do more than read this book. From the beginning—yes, before you even finish this chapter—I recommend getting a journal or notebook, or opening an app on your phone, where you can take notes and start writing ideas down.

I'm going to give you lots of suggestions and share stories from my life with the intention of inspiring you to do things and make changes that will address your issues and help you improve your life. We are all somewhat different. Our life stories, which are unique, are what shape us. As we evolve, we have different needs. As our lives develop and things change, we need to be sensitive to how our needs change and to honor those needs. What works for me may be quite different from what will work for you. I'm sharing what I've learned from both my own experience as well as a lifetime of working in the healing arts and observing my clients.

Begin by making a list of things that nurture you. Include things that are fun, or therapeutic, that help you unwind and recharge. As you read through my chapters, ideas will come to mind. See what jumps out at you, and add them to your journal. Perhaps some of my suggestions will be things you can incorporate right away as a regular part of your life, or my practices may stimulate a few new ideas of your own, unique to you, that will make a difference.

It's important to have things you do daily, weekly, and monthly that replenish the energy you are constantly using. Some of these things may be physical. Some may be mental or emotional. All of them are important.

Part of the secret to radical self-care is discovering exactly what the right recipe is for your own unique set of needs. If you think of your life as a dish at a fabulous culinary feast, what are the ingredients that make it as delectable as possible? What spices and seasonings are going to make it taste both delicious and satisfying?

When the day-to-day business of life starts to claw its way into all our spare time and energy, we can lose our sense of control and thus our inner peace.

And that can drive us nuts.

How Did We Get Like This?

From an early age, we are taught life is a series of tasks and responsibilities we are challenged to complete. When we start going to school and receive homework assignments or tests to study for, we become trained in the art of getting things done. It becomes part of a game, getting the best grades and awards for completing everything to perfection. As children, we recharge by grabbing time to play, making up games with our friends, and disappearing into the world of creativity and imagination.

As we get older, it becomes more difficult to find time for that escape into play as a respite from being the responsible adult. It's a balancing act that continues to get trickier the more responsibilities we accrue. Go to graduate school? Start a business? Become a parent? We live in a culture that rewards accomplishment. And no matter what we have already done, people want to know when we're going to take the next step. Raising a child? When are you going to have another one? Have a good job? When might you expect a promotion? Own a business? What are your plans to expand it? The pressure to always have more, do more, and be more can suck up all of our physical and emotional time and energy. When was the last time you unplugged from the path of accomplishment to feed your spirit?

However swept up we get in becoming responsible people, there is a part of us that yearns for that blissful place we remember from childhood, when life was fun and we had some control and could shape it in a way that deeply fed us. As we grow older, we can, in fact, lose a vital part of who we are when we let too much of our energy get absorbed into work. I have seen people go from being loving, humorous, inspiring personalities to critical, cynical, and disappointed grumps because they lost their juice somewhere along the way.

At a certain point, I realized I had to take charge of making sure I was being nurtured on a regular basis as part of my day-to-day life. I have a strong urge to create and accomplish a lot; I also often crave escaping into pleasure. These two things are sometimes at odds, frequently jockeying for my attention. I need both. And, of course, my time is finite. I started looking at what kinds of self-care practices would give me the balance I need to feel whole and refreshed, so I could return to getting things done with a renewed attitude.

I have a tendency to walk through the house noticing things I have to take care of. My eyes will focus on a stack of magazines that are piling up. Will I ever really have time to read them? I

5

make a mental note that when I have a spare minute, I need to find a permanent place to put them or recycle the ones I know I'm not going to open.

Then I shift my attention to the next article of clutter: mail that needs to be sorted, dealt with, and tossed. There's always mail, right? Every day.

And let's not even start with opening the laptop with the emails and the spam folder. I watch as the daily dose of messages fly into the inbox, quickly scanning to see if anything is important, personal, or interesting. I might start my day by opening one email, reading it, writing a quick response, and then shutting the laptop, thinking, *I can't do this now. I have to eat and get out the door.* So I get up with an uneasy feeling that that I'm letting something important slide as I walk into the kitchen, looking for something easy I can eat before I leave for work. And then I go off to do the best job I can manage. But those emails are waiting, and by the time I return to the laptop, they will have multiplied.

Most people experience some version of this, where our leisure slips away from us, which is why I am bringing it up. It's important to make a point of doing things that take care of our souls as well as clearing out the inbox.

Social media is another place that sucks up our time addictively. Opening those apps becomes a habit that can eat us alive. It has the benefit of helping us keep in touch with a wide range of people, but it is rarely satisfying for the massive amount of time it consumes. I won't say give them up, because that's not realistic, but we do need to limit our time on them.

Radical self-care is about breaking patterns of overworking and taking responsibility for your own well-being. It's making sure you get what you need so you can enjoy your life. If you make these things a part of your regular routine, it will have a positive effect on everything you do and every person you encounter.

Anybody can do it, regardless of their situation. None of these activities require anything more than the will to do them. These are things I've figured out over the course of my life in order to reset my wheels back on the road when they begin to veer too close to the cliff. Your choices may be different. It doesn't matter, really, exactly what the tools are. What does matter is that you commit to changing what you do to incorporate new practices that make you happier and feel better. Once you begin taking the time to prepare a super healthy and delicious lunch you bring to work, this will become a part of your day you look forward to, or maybe your self-care practice is jogging in the park every Saturday morning or beginning your day with fifteen minutes of dancing. Whatever nurturing activities you follow on a regular basis, they become part of your life and are vital aspects of what keep you healthy and happy.

Until these activities become routine, it will require effort to pull yourself away from work to stop and remember to do something nourishing, or you might find that several weeks fly by before you do something nice for yourself again. Building new habits takes time and repetition. Rather than beat yourself up for forgetting to do your self-care practices, try something fun and rewarding to treat yourself instead.

Am I Advocating Selfishness?

Are you cringing a little as you read this? If so, please calm down and take a nice, slow, nurturing breath. Let me explain the difference between selfishness and self-care. The *Merriam-Webster Dictionary* defines *selfishness* as "seeking or concentrating on one's own advantage, pleasure, or well-being without regard for others." Selfish people do not struggle with self-neglect because they automatically make themselves a priority. If you were a selfish person, you would have never picked up this book.

As a massage therapist, my actual survival depends on needing to be needed. When I can help someone relax or relieve their pain, that act, to a certain extent, validates my existence. I know I'm putting this rather dramatically, but I think you get the idea. We all have work that gives us meaning (or, at any rate, that once completed, gives us a sense of satisfaction or self-worth that we accomplished what was expected of us). That's the moment when we feel we can now have that drink, go for a bite to eat, take that walk, or do whatever we do to treat ourselves afterwards.

The problem was, even though I knew the things I liked to do, things that helped me recharge, I wasn't making time to do them often enough. All too frequently, I made excuses, putting off taking care of myself in order to get one more thing done, which always seemed more important.

This can be so deeply ingrained that we don't even realize we're doing it. Often, we wait until illness, addiction, or something destructive sets in before we take a good, hard look at why we're stressed, and by then, things are often at a critical place.

After quite a few decades of working hard to please others (clients, partners, friends, family, you name it), I realized I had to take control of my own well-being. No matter how much I did, it never felt like enough. I had goals that were difficult to attain, and even when I met them, they didn't satisfy me like I thought they would. Basically, I had bought into our very driven culture that I spoke about earlier, even though I had carved out a professional niche in the field of relaxation. Ironic, isn't it?

For example, journal writing has become a form of therapy for me. I have kept a notebook of some kind since I was a teenager. I like to go off somewhere away from my home to write. That way, I don't become distracted by things needing my attention. I'll go to a coffee shop or, if the weather's nice, an outdoor café, or even a bench in the park. Once I'm there and open my journal, I enter another world where I can breathe a deep sigh of relief, because now I have set aside some time just for me. This has become my signal to myself that I am on a break, and I have been doing this for so many years, it works like magic. The hardest part is pulling myself away from my responsibilities, grabbing my journal, and scurrying out the door. But once I've done that, it's heaven.

Now when I am uncomfortable or stressed, I know what I need to do to make the changes my soul is craving. I can't depend on anyone else to understand the subtle things I need, and frankly, I wouldn't want to put that pressure on anyone else. I love the feeling of being self-sufficient, knowing I have everything I need to take care of myself and I'm the one in control of making that happen.

We can wrench ourselves away from the hamster wheel and find the quiet time necessary to reset our equilibrium. Sometimes, radical self-care takes a huge effort to get started. That's why it's called radical.

CHAPTER 2

Saving My Life with Self-Care

Self-care has been my own spiritual practice of physical, mental, and emotional survival.

As a massage therapist, having had my own practice, owning a day spa, and working at high-end resorts, I know this scenario of uncontrollable giving behavior very well. I spent my days giving massages and listening to the stories from my clients, which were often like talk therapy sessions. I loved my work and found it deeply meaningful, but I sometimes found it was hard for me to recharge. There was always so much to do and someone who needed my attention. In my solo practice, I worked alone and had to do everything. When I opened the day spa, it brought in a lot more money, but it added more stress because I not only had a larger business to handle, but I had a staff of people to manage who had their own problems that interfered with the smooth running of the business. I was always dealing with some conflict, handling a stressful situation, or managing things that were necessary in order to keep the business going. I was hardly ever calm, rarely relaxed. That's when I started developing strategies for coping. I enlisted the aid of other professionals in the healing arts to help me, as well as consultants skilled in the art of helping small business owners. Having a support system of other skilled professionals was a big help on the road to self-preservation because these people understood the challenges I was dealing with; they validated everything I was experiencing. I also had self-help books I kept at work to read whenever I had an hour that wasn't booked, and I used that time to learn about things I could do that were healing.

Having success and being profitable was not enough. I also had to stay sane and be able to enjoy my life, or it was not worth it. My need for a less complicated life eventually motivated me to sell the day spa and instead work at resorts, where I could just come to work, massage a few people, and go home, leaving the complexities of running the business to someone else. That choice in itself, selling my busy day spa, was an act of self-care. An outsider might question why I would leave a successful, profitable business. But it was making my life more complicated than I wanted it to be. I loved the creative aspect of building a business exactly the way I imagined it and developing skills of fostering a family-like environment for my staff, but eventually, it felt like too much.

Since I'm more of a pleaser type of person, it was uncomfortable for me to be the boss, where I had to make rules and make sure those rules were followed. I also had to handle conflicts between coworkers and issues with difficult clients, all while dealing with the marketing, the accounting, fixing things that broke, and keeping everything running smoothly. It was a lot. Since it was open seven days a week, I could get a call at any time about a problem that needed to be addressed. I never felt free of the needs and worries of keeping the spa going. Being part of groups with other small business owners was one way I found help and resources that gave me support. In fact, it was validating because other people in similar positions felt the same way I did. But eventually, I undertook the ultimate act of self-care and sold the business, removing a significant weight from my emotional back.

Here's an example of how the practices I am about to share with you played out in my life:

In 2008, the economy was tanking, and it was quite hard to make money at the resort where I was working. People had stopped indulging in discretionary activities. I decided to change careers and get training in something more versatile, in the health care industry. I enrolled in a two-year medical imaging program at the local junior college so I could become a certified radiologic technologist. With that degree, I could work in a hospital, performing x-rays and other diagnostic modalities, giving me some measure of job security. This environment did not suit me at all. It was so different from working in the soothing spa environment I was used to. From the beginning of the medical training, I was stressed. I do not like being told what to do, but there, every breath I took was micromanaged by the hospital staff. This had me in a constant state of anxiety, and I spent every day with my stomach tightly clenched as I performed each task to the best of my ability. I justified this stress as part of the package of learning a skill that was necessary for my financial survival.

I was always looking for ways to make my life more palatable. Since I put in ten-hour days, including my commute, there wasn't much time to recharge. Thus, I had to find small ways throughout the day to calm my nerves. When I was doing a rotation at the level 1 trauma hospital, they had us park in a lot about half a mile away and sent buses back and forth, shuttling people to and from the hospital. It was September, and summer was still hanging on. During the day, the temperatures reached into the 90s, but early in the morning, when I got to the parking lot around 6:30, it was still pleasantly cool. I decided that rather than take the bus, I would walk. This gave me a nice, slow start to the day. I had twenty minutes to get centered while I strolled down to the large hospital.

I was training in the angiography lab, where heart patients had stents inserted into their arteries. As I walked, taking in the cool morning air, I savored every moment of freedom I had before reaching the large facility. I loved that feeling and treasured every instant. No one was telling me what to do. Nothing was being demanded of me. I walked past rows of large trees and watched the way their branches and leaves made shapes against the sky. Every leaf was a work of art. My breathing slowed, as I continued down the street towards the hospital. By the time I arrived, I was not only relaxed, but felt empowered and ready for whatever would be asked of me.

One day as I was walking, someone on a motorcycle pulled up alongside me. It was Rob, the tech who was training me.

"How come you're not on the bus?" he asked.

"I like walking," I said.

I knew this was not something regulated by the hospital. I had the freedom to walk if I wanted to. My accountability didn't begin until I pressed the code and walked through the door to the angiography lab.

"Hop on," he said, gesturing to the back of his bike.

Well, it wasn't part of my plan, but I didn't want to be rude. Besides, riding on the back of a bike is fun, so I jumped on behind him, and within a few minutes, we arrived.

As we slid off, he looked at me curiously.

"You're not like other people," he said with a grin.

I gave him a big smile. No, I'm not. And for a moment, I felt a wave of excitement, because in that knowing look, I saw Rob understood me.

Little Life Hacks Keep Me Sane

Whatever I am doing, I try to figure out a way to make it more fun and pleasurable or, depending on what it is, more tolerable. There are so many things we have to do, whether we like it or not, so I'm always looking for ways to soften the experience. That's the part where we have some measure of control.

When it was time to break for lunch, we all went to the hospital cafeteria. I liked to sit outside at a table, near trees or plants. Those hospitals have no idea what a huge deal it was to me, to be able to have a break outside and see something green growing. I also brought my own bowl for my food. I packed a handmade piece of stoneware pottery in my lunch box; I purchased it at an art show, and it made my food so much more enjoyable than using one of the cafeteria's cardboard plates. I know people looked at me strangely as I pulled out the bowl with its blue and light grey patterns and poured my salad into it, but I didn't care.

Little things like that helped me reclaim some of my experience and make it my own, something I desperately needed. If I could, I swear I would have pulled out a little bud vase and pop a flower into it. Any little addition of nature, art, or beauty added some delight and helped me feel like I was there on my own terms. Whenever I had to do something I didn't want to, these little life hacks went a long way toward helping me cope.

While I was in the Medical Imaging Program, every Sunday, I took myself out to a French bakery that was a ten-minute walk from my house. I got a cinnamon walnut croissant, had a cup of Earl Grey tea, and wrote in my journal. Every Sunday. It was my opportunity to unwind and rant about all the crazy things that happened during the week in class and at the hospital. I ended each entry with a list of things I was grateful for and a list of things I was praying for. I have been doing these things forever.

These little self-care practices saved my life.

How Our Past Shapes Us

Let me explain. I grew up with a critical mother who was difficult to please. I needed that mother-love and was always trying to get her approval. She wanted the best for me and had a really specific criteria of what that was. I worked hard at doing the things I was told to do: getting high grades, giving my all to dance recitals, and that sort of thing. It was never enough, and I grew up with an insatiable habit of giving and trying to please others.

This led me to the massage career, which I found incredibly rewarding because my job consisted of doing things that made people happy. Every person I worked on felt better afterwards and thanked me. A lifetime of needing to please was finally rewarded. It was, however, hard for me to know when I needed to stop giving to others and when it was time to take care of myself.

I learned many people in the healing arts tend to be sensitive people who get burned out when they spend too much energy taking care of others and not enough time taking care of themselves. There are many industries where this is the case. Health care workers, both in hospitals and private practice, experience this. Teachers know this well, as they have to teach, create curriculums, grade papers and tests, and be there for the special requests of their students.

When you work in a job where people rely on you for help, you must have good boundaries. I learned this eventually, and it's why I've devoted a whole chapter to it. In the beginning of my career, I took pride in being needed, but I overdid it. I took care of my house, my partner, my parents, my friends. I once went to a personal growth workshop where the facilitator described this as "uncontrollable giving behavior." Yup, she nailed it.

This is what happened. I was the person people could count on, but inside, I was becoming quite worn out. I knew this was unhealthy, and I had to figure out some new habits. Although I know what to do in order to help get refreshed, that falls away when I get too busy and have too much to squeeze into a limited amount of time. During periods of my life when I wasn't working much and had lots of discretionary time, it was easier to incorporate restorative moments into my schedule. However, when I was busy, I found I had to be more systematic about practices for recharging. I started writing about them on my blog, "As the Spirit Moves Me," as a way of reinforcing better habits. As I shared the blog posts, I realized this resonated with quite a lot of other people. I decided to use the blog posts about self-care practices as a blueprint for this book. One of the things that helps when you're going through something challenging is to learn you're not alone. I learned many people could identify with the need for self-care practices, and that motivated me to expand on this.

There are many reasons why we feel the need to be available to others and feel guilty when we take time for ourselves. It could be how we get our sense of self-worth. When people need us, we feel valuable. So helping others reinforces that feeling of being important. It can also be how we define being a good person as opposed to being a selfish one. And it can be much more complicated than that, going back to early childhood issues. But whatever the reason, getting lost in a cycle of depletion can lead to ill health and a bad attitude.

When we wear ourselves out, we lose the vitality that boosts our immune system and are more prone to illness. In addition to being more vulnerable to physical ills, we are also susceptible to depression and health problems caused by fatigue and emotional breakdown.

When we become too dependent on the approval of others for our self-esteem, it's hard to ever feel truly full. We cannot do enough. There is not enough praise in the whole world. And yet, many of us continue this pattern because that is how we were raised, whether it came from our parents, teachers, or people we met along the way. We are trained to try to get the highest grades, win at sports, get into the best schools, date the sexiest or most successful person we can find, make a lot of money, get a prestigious job, wear fashionable clothing, and win awards for what we do. The list goes on and on about how we get our self-worth from our sense of accomplishment and how we appear to others.

That is why self-care is so critical.

Reclaiming Your Life

Rather than focus on how others see you, in order to be a good person and feel worthy, it's necessary to disconnect from the outside world and tune in to your deepest needs. I am talking about being your own best friend, as you are the only one who really understands what will make you feel good. It's up to you to schedule time to restore your spirit, rest, and do the things that nourish you. When you take charge of your life like this, it is incredibly empowering. You start to love and appreciate yourself just as much as all the people you have been helping, because now, you get to be on the receiving end. And the cool thing is that when your own needs are met, you have so much more energy to give to others. You don't have to fake it.

The challenge is keeping it up. This isn't anything new. It isn't as though I go for years with no self-care. It can, however, be inconsistent. I will take a trip to a woodsy cabin and spend three days curled up with a book, making some delectable food to live off of and catching up on my sleep. And then I will return and plunge back into my life relentlessly, waiting for the next getaway, which may be months or even a whole year off.

Although vacations or a weekend getaway can be quite restorative, we need to do things regularly. We need to have daily practices that can help us get back into balance.

This book helps define those activities I have found to be most helpful, and I encourage you, just as I do, to incorporate them into your life on a daily and weekly basis. You don't save up your hunger and eat a gigantic meal once a month. And you can't save up your need to recharge like that, either. Think of it as feeding your soul, just like you feed your tummy. You need those calories at regular intervals in order to keep going and remain physically healthy. Your spirit needs that nourishment on a regular basis too. I'm sure there are many things you already do to replenish yourself throughout your day. This is about being more conscious of them, defining them, and making sure you are doing them more regularly.

You may find making a schedule to incorporate regular practices helps you to actually do them. Otherwise, you could read this book and think, *Yeah, that sounds like a good idea,* but never make any changes. I understand how easy it is to put things off, especially when there are pressing things and people requiring your immediate attention. Taking care of yourself can seem like something indulgent, something to do after you get everything else done. But the thing is, you will never get everything else done. So please just own up to that right off the bat. You cannot wait until everything on the to-do list is checked off before you take time for yourself.

As you go through the self-care chapters, think about the ways you can incorporate these things into your own life and how each idea applies to you. Tweak them to suit your own lifestyle.

Some of the suggestions in this book may require large chunks of time if, for example, you need to take a vacation or go away for the weekend. Whereas the chapter on "A Hedonist's Guide to Healthy Eating" doesn't take any extra time at all; it's just a mindful approach to what you're already doing. The benefit of taking care with your eating in a way that makes you feel better can be enormous. In fact, these practices are mostly about making small changes that have huge returns.

I have been using many of these practices, such as journaling, creativity, and good financial management, throughout my life, for as long as I can remember. Whereas others, like resting and finding more time, are more of a challenge. I wrote this book because I see so many stressed-out people and thought it would be helpful to simplify these steps so people could live more rewarding lives.

Abraham Maslow's Hierarchy of Needs

In 1943, psychologist Abraham Maslow presented a paper on the human hierarchy of needs; his work has become incorporated into current psychology practice. It is the awareness that humans have many levels of needs, from the most basic survival needs of food, water, and physical accommodation to emotional and spiritual needs, like needing to feel we have a purpose and our lives are meaningful.

That last need I mention, a craving to have a purpose, or the need to be needed, can be so strong, we can go overboard trying to make sure what we do has value. Enough value. Am I good enough? Do people like me? Do they think I'm important? Do I shine? These are the underlying reasons people overwork themselves to be seen as a someone who has something to offer. It is a basic human need to feel we fit in and we are needed. People go about this in various ways: putting in a lot of hours at work, making public appearances and community donations, winning awards and levels of high achievement, whether it's at a job, in sports, or in the arts. Below is the famous pyramid of Maslow's needs, which shows their importance, from the most basic physiological needs for survival to the most internal, intellectual, and spiritual, regarding our higher purpose. All are important. The chapters of this book feature practices that address all of these needs.

This chart shows why we are complex individuals. Please use this list to help understand why you feel the way you do and to discover how you may satisfy some deep longings.

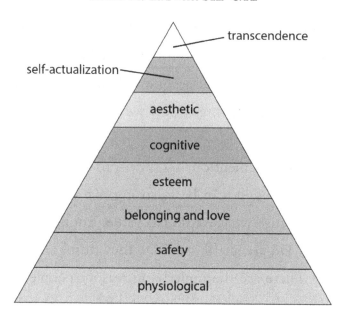

We don't always view the higher levels as needs, but they are just as important to our survival. Although the physical needs are obvious, when the psychological needs of fitting in, being valued, and feeling appreciated are not met, that can result in destructive behaviors. People use drugs, alcohol, and other practices to escape feeling like they aren't measuring up to the standard we have in our minds. Of course, the escape is only temporary, and we can get stuck in a destructive cycle of short-term escape, damaging backlash, and repeating the pattern until there's an inevitable crash.

If we don't have some sort of guidance, we don't know what to do. It is challenging when we get the message, through advertisements, movies, and the media, that the most important thing is to be the best, the sexiest, the smartest, the winner of the trophy or the medal or the award.

I have found it quite enlightening to read the memoirs of famous people and learn about their struggles. One learns the person we see on the TV screen is not necessarily the same one who goes home at the end of the day. And the more we achieve, the higher the expectations become for what we will do next. This becomes an endless cycle of pressure. It can be rewarding and exciting too, depending on how you view it.

I learned a really important lesson that is the essence of what I want to share with you:

Happiness doesn't come from how others see you, but from how you see yourself. If you use the attention of others, whether that's your family, friends, or coworkers, or in the case of a famous person, the media and the public, in order to feel good about yourself, you will always feel like you're not enough, and you could do better, or you have a high bar to maintain, and keeping it up can be exhausting.

The real secret to happiness is to feel whole and complete within yourself. The purpose of this book is to help you get there.

CHAPTER 3

Wholeness: Being Your
Own Best Friend

How often do you judge yourself by how you look to others? Do you take stock of your friends and acquaintances, take inventory of your accomplishments, or make a mental list of things that sum up your value? Do you fret about how clean your home is? Do you look in the mirror critically, wondering if you should change your hair style or lose weight? Do you worry about your social life being active enough?

We can be our own worst critic. We look at the calendar, examining our activities. Are we using our time wisely? Are we spending too much time on social media so that before we know it, our break is over?

Two important questions: What should you be doing? And what does your soul crave?

I deeply believe that in one sense, we are all we've really got. Of course, we have people we're close to, and we need them, but we can't always count on them. They might be busy or out of town when we really need to talk, or maybe they don't want to go with us for a walk on the beach or out to lunch at the new tapas restaurant. Friends are wonderful and necessary, but we can't depend on them always being there for us, because ultimately, they have to be there for themselves. It's great when our desires and their availability overlap, but that's not always going to happen. Ultimately, we are the only ones we can always truly count on.

Fitting In

It is important to feel like we belong, that there's a place for us here in the world, specifically, in the community where we live. This may be one of the biggest psychological issues of human life. When we are part of something we enjoy, we feel good. When we have a role to play where we're needed, whether it's at a job or when we're helping someone, we feel valuable. We feel connected when we're with a group of friends, in a class we're taking, volunteering for a community project, a member of a meaningful organization, or whatever home is at the moment.

Feeling like we're part of something important to us is essential to human existence. It's why there were tribes in ancient cultures. It's why some people feel suspicious of people who are different from them or don't share their history. It's why people cling to family or to an organization they are a part of. Feeling like we fit and belong is essential to feeling okay about ourselves and our existence. We gravitate to like-minded groups of people. We have expressions like "these are my people." Being part of these groups helps give us a safe space in which to thrive. We know we're okay because we fit in with these people who think like us, like the same things we like, agree with us about things that we consider critical.

Sometimes, it can be hard to feel like we fit in because there's so much going on all the time, it's easy to feel left out. Even if we grow up in a close family, which not everyone does, once we go out into the world, we encounter so many different possibilities of things we can do. It can be confusing trying to figure out where we fit the best. Maybe we like certain people but worry they won't like us back. Maybe we want to be part of a group, but when we try to engage, we don't feel truly accepted. Perhaps we are part of a group of friends when we are in school, but then we graduate. People move away for jobs, for continuing education, for romantic relationships, and those connections from grade school or high school or college can weaken or dissolve. Sometimes, you may realize you don't really feel part of any group at the moment.

This can be the source of severe angst, anxiety, and depression.

Inward versus Outward Focus

This is why I love the concept of being your own best friend. Being able to always take care of your needs and wants is a big deal. It's not the way most of us were brought up, so it takes practice. It takes a different way of thinking about yourself and your life. You may not have anything scheduled on your day off, so that's an opportunity to do something you want. Maybe you can take a day trip to a nearby town, or go for a walk in a park or to the beach, or try a new restaurant. Having dates with yourself can be a lot of fun. You can decide what you want to do, and you don't have to convince anyone else to go along with it.

The topics I'm writing about in this book come from a lifetime of realizing this. Throughout my life, I have figured out ways to take care of myself so I could manage my life without relying too much on others.

Being your own best friend is the key. Knowing you can rely on yourself for much of what you need, or at least trusting yourself to manage the challenges, gives you a certain strength and autonomy. You know you can trust yourself to get your needs met. This is wholeness. This is gold.

CHAPTER 4

Step 1. Time: Our Most Precious Resource

Can I borrow some of your time? I'm a little short.

It doesn't really work that way, does it? Whereas I have a savings account with money I can accumulate until I'm ready to spend it, time is always passing. It is constantly being spent, whether it's on something I absolutely love, dealing with necessities, indulging in a bit of foolishness, or doing something I don't like.

I have come to value time as the most precious thing we have. The importance of being mindful about how we spend it is a critical practice.

How Do You Spend Your Time?

Do you save it up for juicy indulgences of pleasure? Do you manage your life efficiently so you have the most amount of time for the things you really love to do? Do you take breaks regularly so you have a chance relax and reset your energy? Do you consider going out with friends a break? Or do you get more recharge time doing something quietly alone?

Perhaps you blow those extra hours frivolously, not even realizing where they went, until you notice that suddenly, you are all out of time.

This is something I have become acutely aware of. It's like a secret treasure that has been there all along, but I never even paid much attention to.

This became very obvious to me, when I struggled to fit in all the things I wanted to do: all the projects I wanted to accomplish, the friends I wanted to keep up with, and the realization that I had very little breathing space for myself. There was so little unscheduled time. I rarely had days where there was no agenda, no appointments, no dates with friends, and no errands.

I realized having enough alone time is an unmet need. And how luxurious it felt whenever I had a few hours just to myself, with nothing in particular I had to get done. I especially loved it when I had a day or two that were completely free. How insanely delicious that was. I would try to hang on to it, as the minutes slipped by, until it was over, and I had to go to work or move on to the next thing. I would look into the future, wondering when the next block of uninterrupted privacy would emerge. And that's when I started regarding my time as a very precious resource that needed budgeting, just like my money.

I decided to set aside blocks of time to take getaways by myself, with two or three days at a time that were just for me. My goal was to have a getaway once a month. That wasn't always possible, but each time I did this, it became clear how valuable it was. I like to go to the north coast of California, about two hours from where I live, and stay someplace quiet. There's a spot on an ocean bluff, where I can take hikes and be soothed by nature. I use this time for my writing, as well as for indulging in things that are impossible in a busy household, such as long bouts of reading.

On my solo getaways, sometimes, I stay in bed until noon, lost in a good book. It's hard to even describe how heavenly that is. I try not to have too many goals (like getting several chapters of my book written) because I don't want to turn my getaway into another form of pressure. However, I do find I need this quiet time in order to write. So I make it a priority. In order not to feel stressed by my writing goals, I balance the writing time with hikes and other indulgences. I usually write in the morning, then go out for a hike in the afternoon and do a little more writing before I eat dinner. After dinner, I build a fire, read books, and just relax. That way, I'm getting my creative work done and still have time to unwind. My home is more distracting, since I live with people and several pets. I usually have to go to a coffee shop if I want to write without being interrupted. But during my getaways, I get a lot more done.

Once I started going away, I realized what a gift I was giving myself. I think I value this sacred time almost more than anything else.

What are the things you need to set aside time for? Are you getting enough of the things you really crave? Make a list of things you want to make room for in your schedule. As you write things down, note how frequently you are able to do them and which activities you need to make more room for. What are some ways you unplug and relax? What activities do you find soothing? What is your favorite thing to do when you're craving a real break?

What Is a Waste of Time?

Wasting time can be compared to mindless eating. You know how you regret eating something that wasn't worth the calories? Spending time doing things you don't enjoy and aren't required to do is kind of like that. Are there things in your life you've signed up for out of obligation that you could drop? I'll bet there are many. We agree to many things in order to be kind or helpful, or because we feel expected to do so. If we are committing to too much, especially things we don't want to do, we need to learn to decline. Regardless of how much someone else wants us to do something, having integrity with ourselves about what we commit to is more important. Otherwise, we become resentful.

This is a self-care practice that clearly requires us to prioritize what is important and what isn't. We are constantly faced with choices about how we spend our discretionary time, and this is when we need to be really honest with ourselves. Along with the need for rest, we need to feel good about how we spend our time, or we will burn out.

Just like we can't eat everything on the menu, we can't do everything that presents itself to us. Some things have to be postponed, and others will be shelved in favor of something more satisfying.

This can be a very difficult practice. It can be hard to say no. It also can be hard to understand what our motivation is for doing the things we agree to. Just like managing food or money, we need to be mindful about what we are doing and why, or suddenly, we wonder how our time disappeared so quickly. Where did it go?

Set Priorities

First, take a look at how things are scheduled in your week or month, so you can see where your time is going. Just like mapping out a budget or planning meals, look at what changes you can make so you can spend the majority of your discretionary time doing things you most value.

Just like paying the bills comes before splurges, your work, family, and other commitments are set on your schedule. After that, there is probably quite a bit that is negotiable. There will always be trade-offs. Some weeks will be more about necessities and others more about things that feed your soul.

One of the things I did was hire people to clean my house and mow my backyard. These are two things I didn't really mind doing, but I certainly didn't enjoy, and they took up enough time that it sucked up the better part of a day. I found people who could do these things at a price I could afford, and it went a long way to freeing me up so I had both the time and the energy to work on things I really valued.

Another thing I did was I stopped going to a community group I wasn't enjoying. In the beginning, it sounded perfect. I've been part of many groups like that at various times. But this particular group did not work for me. I'm not sure exactly what it was. I just know on the day of each meeting, I would feel very tired and reluctant about going. Afterwards, I would leave, feeling I didn't get that much out of it, and I didn't want to go anymore. It was hard to drop out, though, since I cared about many of the people in the group. I didn't want to hurt anyone's feelings. But these gatherings were not feeding me. I was not enjoying them.

I finally had to be honest with myself that the time spent there was not worth it. This can be the case with a class you might sign up for that you think will be fun but doesn't end up meeting your expectations. What do you do, then? Do you keep going because you committed to it? This is when you have to listen to your inner voice and acknowledge that continuing to do something that is optional isn't worth it if you aren't enjoying it.

Once you start looking at your time in this new way, you'll find you are more careful about the plans you make. You will start setting aside time for the things you really want to do, just like I do with my getaways. I find it's helpful to put my dates with myself on the calendar. That way, there isn't an empty block of time that can be filled with something else. It may seem odd to see places in the calendar that say, "Walk in the park" or "Go to café and journal." But it will also make you smile. There's nothing wrong with being odd. Trust me.

Some Things to Consider

How much time do you need for yourself? Do you have creative projects you are working on? When do you schedule time for them?

How is your social life? Are you spending time with the people you most want to see? Is your social life feeding your soul?

What about community involvement? Is this something you find rewarding? This can be anything from participating in sports, being part of local theater, or even engaging in political activism. It's being involved with activities that involve other people and are meaningful to you.

What is not working? Take a long look at all the things you are doing, and evaluate which ones you are happy to be doing and which ones feel more like an obligation. Which ones feel worth it? Which ones can you give. up?

Do you crave alone time? Some people do. Some don't. I absolutely need big chunks of it. If this is something that helps you recharge, make sure you are getting it frequently. It can be a few hours here and there, and occasionally whole days all to yourself.

The Biggest Question of All

What is most important to you? It all comes down to that. What is going to give you the most satisfaction from your life?

Whether it's something serious like being on the board of your community environmental organization or something creative like being part of your local theater, or a solo activity like a drive to the beach or a park, choose whatever makes your life feel most worthwhile. Be truly honest with yourself. This isn't about doing things because you get admiration or approval from others. Unless it really rocks your world, it isn't worth devoting your precious, discretionary time to it.

This is about honoring your relationship to yourself in a way that no one else can, even the people who deeply love you, because no one else knows how you feel and what nurtures you like you do. No one else notices or cares when you run out of time. Nobody feels it but you. No one can give it to you but your own careful planning.

And it costs absolutely nothing. Except mindfulness.

Exercises to Get More Time

- Block off time on your calendar in order to set aside some time for yourself, whether it's to work on a specific project or to have a date with yourself. It's important to put it on the schedule so that time remains free just for you.

- Make a list of things that eat up your time and are not worth it. The intent is to become aware of time you spend that feels wasted, so you can stop yourself before you get sucked into something you can do without.

- Make a list of things you want time for. What is the most valuable activity to you, in terms of how you might spend discretionary time? It can even be taking a nap, if you're feeling exhausted and overwhelmed.

CHAPTER 5

Step 2. Journaling as a Regular Practice

Go Ahead, Let it Out

Journaling can be a form of therapy.

There is so much we hold inside, unexpressed. Sometimes, we're like an overly full container about to explode. Even with people to talk to, such as a partner, spouse, or close friend, we have to be mindful of how much we share. As much as people love us, there is a limit to how much our need to process our thoughts can intrude on them, without wearing them out.

On the other hand, if we keep too much conflict inside us, it can make us sick. We have to let it out somehow.

Journaling is a fabulous tool for this. The type of journaling I am suggesting is something to be kept private. It's your safe, secret space. You can write anything. You can swear, you can be mean, you can be ugly, you can whine. You can be all the things that are socially unacceptable, or you can use it as an opportunity to debate the pros and cons of something you are involved in or about to do. There's no limit to the way a journal can be used. It's a tool to connect with yourself and give a voice to the thoughts and feelings that are swirling around inside.

I started journaling when I was in high school. I was going through that awkward period of trying to figure out who I was and how I fit in with my peers and with the world. I used spiral notebooks, scribbling thoughts, poetry, and anything I felt like saying. It was my first foray into writing, using the written word to express myself. In the beginning, I didn't separate journaling from other writing projects, so sometimes, my ramblings became the beginnings of creative writing pieces.

Over the years, I ritualized the process. I bought blank books for the specific purpose of keeping a private journal, relishing moments when I could take some time for myself and pour everything out. This ritual became a time of great relief, when I could be alone with my thoughts and explore them through writing.

Julia Cameron, author of *The Artist's Way*, recommends writing three pages every morning before doing anything else. In her experience, it clears the mind, helps you process and release thoughts that are holding you back, and makes way for new and creative ideas. She insists that when you let go of the resistance to doing it, the practice can change your life. Although I found her passion for this validating, I prefer writing later in the day and do it two or three times a week, instead of daily.

On days when I can get an early start, I write first thing in the morning. But when I have to get out the door early, I postpone my journaling until later.

Finding Your Place

There is no right or wrong way to journal. As long as you are clear that this is private, you can feel safe to write anything. Experiment with writing daily, as Julia Cameron recommends. You may find your rhythm for this kind of writing is weekly or on your lunch break at work, if that turns out to be the best time. You may find writing while sitting in bed is most comfortable, when you are cozy and disconnected from the outer world, either first thing in the morning or last thing at night.

Experiment with writing in different environments at different intervals to see what resonates best for you. Remember, this is solely for your own benefit. As I share my experience, use it as a guideline, but trust that you will find your own way of using this practice.

I like to go someplace away from home to write in my journal. For me, getting away from the environment where I am distracted by all the things I am responsible for helps me let go and focus more easily. When I write at home, since I live in a busy household, I know I could be interrupted at any moment, and one part of my brain is always on guard.

Opportunities to journal are often an excuse to take myself on a little break. Sometimes, I combine it with going for a walk. There is a bakery café a twenty-minute walk from my house that I like to go to, get in an early morning walk, sit, and write for half an hour while having some tea and a cookie, and then walk home. It's a charming bakery that doesn't mind having people sitting with laptops open, so I feel free to pull out my journal and disappear into it. They have great music channels on the sound system, which lends itself to a comforting atmosphere. Oldies from my past come on, which remind me of old times that make me smile.

Another favorite place is a market with a nice deli that has tables and chairs set up outside. I like to sit under the covered awning with iced tea and a snack from the shop. When the weather is nice, I go there. It's situated in a quiet, upscale neighborhood, surrounded by large trees and planter boxes overflowing with potted geraniums and poppies. It's such a peaceful, quiet spot that it's easy to get lost in the thoughts I pour into my journal.

Experiment with different places, and see how you like them. Mainly, you want places that don't have distractions so you can focus inwardly and disappear into your inner world, pouring everything out into your journal. Once you start writing things down, it takes the edge off of issues that have been spinning in your head. Often, there are things going on in our lives that we're trying to sort out. Dilemmas. Problems. Relationships. And many things we really can't talk about with anyone else. Writing in your journal gives you an opportunity to communicate what you're thinking and feeling; it can be very freeing, as it relieves a hidden emotional weight from your psyche.

When I have a free afternoon, I take day trips out to the coast or to nearby towns that have special little spots to have a meal while writing in my journal. One of these places is in Duncan's Mills, a tiny town one block long on the way to the coast. They have a bakery that makes pizza as well as sweets, so sometimes I go there for lunch. There is a garden out back with comfortable seating that is surrounded by trees. Everywhere I look, it's green. It's almost like being in a woodsy backyard.

Sometimes I grab my journal, hop in the car, and go to a spot right where the Russian River meets the ocean in Jenner, a place called Café Aquatica. It's a tiny coffee shop that makes simple lunches, housed in a weathered, wooden shack. They have Adirondack-style seats outside next to small tables, so I can lean back and watch the river flow by while I eat, drink coffee, and write. People occasionally paddle by in canoes. The ocean is visible just beyond the river, and it's so peaceful to watch the seagulls fly by across the ripples of water.

These are all casual places that don't seem to mind me sitting and writing, as long as I've purchased something. Choosing to bring my journal to one of these places is an excuse to treat myself to more than just writing. Being in a different environment helps me get away from my routine, and gives me a different perspective. Even if it's just an hour or two, it makes a big difference.

Choosing Your Voice

One way to get started is to imagine you are talking to someone when you write. Sometimes, I imagine I am one part of myself talking to another part. It might be my inner wise woman giving me advice. Another time, I might be wailing at God or a higher power, asking them for help.

One day, I was on my way up the coast (I talk about my coastal trips a lot; they are a huge part of my self-care practice). I usually stop at a favorite place for lunch on the way up, get a table with a nice view of the ocean, and use that time to write in my journal as I eat. I am often bursting with things to write about. Most likely, inner pressure has been building up, waiting for its chance to escape to freedom.

On this particular day, I was feeling rather fraught about my writing and creative practices. I wasn't sure if I was doing the right thing. I wasn't sure what I should be doing, what direction to go in. I have about five books I've started writing, some of them even completed but in dire need of massive editing and rewriting. On that day, I was having one of those "What is the purpose of my life?" moments. I treated myself to a light lunch at the Sea Ranch Lodge, an upscale restaurant that is part of a large, sprawling development of vacation homes that cover a large stretch of the coast. As I dug into my roasted beet and goat cheese salad, I hoped the waitress wouldn't mind me scribbling away as I ate. It was not crowded, and I don't think anyone cared.

I decided to let my journal writing be a prayer.

"Dear God, Goddess, Higher Power, Spirit, or whomever you're calling yourself these days, please come and be with me right now. I need your help. I don't know what I should be doing. I don't know what will make me happy. I need a sign. I really need help in a big way. I don't know what to do, and I feel nothing but angst no matter what I focus on. Please, please, please give me a sign."

I was nearly crying at that point. Heaven only knows what the waitress must have thought of me, this odd little woman eating her salad and writing furiously in her book, with, I can only imagine, the most intense, pained expression on her face. I wrote until I felt calmer, having released some deep emotions, paid my bill, and then continued another few miles north on the coast highway to my destination.

When I pulled into town, I decided to stop in at the independent bookstore to see if there was anything good I could curl up with and get lost in for a few days. I started to browse through their section of memoirs and biographies. I love books with stories about how real people got through hard, crazy times. While I was looking through the books, one of the employees sat down near me with a large cardboard box full of paperbacks. I glanced down at the box of books, and in there, I saw Elizabeth Gilbert's *Big Magic*, a book about creativity and the creative process. This was May 2015, and I knew *Big Magic* was not due for release until September.

"Wow," I exclaimed. "I see you have Elizabeth Gilbert's new book, but I thought it wasn't being released until September. Can I take a peek at it? I can't wait until it's for sale. I promise I'll buy my copy here."

The clerk explained that the stores get early releases to familiarize them with the upcoming books. She handed me the book and said between now and the time of the actual release, many things could be changed, edited, or rewritten. This wasn't necessarily the finished product. I opened the book; aware I was holding a treasure most of the world had not yet seen. I started reading and became absorbed. After finishing the first chapter, I put it back in the box, saying if I read any more, I wouldn't be able to put it down. The clerk smiled, picked up her box of books, and disappeared.

A few minutes later, she came back, handed me *Big Magic*, and said, "Here. Just take it. I talked to the owner, and he said you could have it."

"Really? Oh, my God. Well, let me pay you for it."

"No, we can't charge for it. It's not the final copy. Just take it."

I was stunned. I couldn't believe what was happening. I realized the clerk intended for me to take the book and leave. Right away. I rose, holding the book I had been leafing through right before this happened, bought it, and clutching the two books, left the store. I got to my car and sat for a few minutes, trying to digest what had just happened. I had just been given a book that was not yet available for sale to the public. It was a book on creativity, exactly what I had been trying to process in my journal. It talked about the importance of listening to your inner voice. It talked about the value of following your curiosity without putting pressure on yourself or your creativity to bring in money or have to be any sort of objective success. Creativity for creativity's sake. I spent the next two days wrapped up in bed, snacking on fruit, cheese, and graham crackers, reading *Big Magic*. It answered my questions. It was the response to my prayer. True story.

Your Journal Can Be a Free Therapist

Other times, I pretend I am having a written therapy session and write as though I am talking to a wise, caring person. It's a great way to process through something that has been churning inside. If I feel stuck, like my thoughts are going in circles, it often helps me understand what's going on. I pretend I'm talking to a healer. Sometimes, I picture a specific person who helped me at one time. I might even write down questions, such as, "What do you think about that?" Sometimes, they respond back with answers. My inner wise voice pipes in, giving me advice or reminding me of some nugget I seem to have momentarily forgotten.

Thoughts and brilliant insights can suddenly come up, just like when you are talking to a therapist, and suddenly, you have ideas that surprise you, because for the first time, you are actually verbalizing a feeling. The same sorts of light bulbs go off when journal writing.

At times like these, writing can help clarify what's going on. There might be something bugging me that isn't exactly clear, but I can feel myself reacting to it. I can't solve the problem if I don't know what it is. I can't focus on it with my thoughts while I'm doing other things because I'm too distracted. When I take a break and go someplace quiet, where I have the tranquility to write uninterrupted in the journal, the thoughts and feelings become words on the page, and I can finally get a clearer picture of my situation.

All for the price of a cup of tea.

Journaling as Meditation

When I write in my journal, much of the time, I am capturing a snapshot of the present moment. I often begin by describing where I am.

"Today I am at the Café Des Croissants, sitting in the back, where I am out of the way of the people pushing their way towards the front counter. Van Morrison is coming through the sound system loud and clear, and for a moment, it is like being in another place, another time."

Or "I finally made it out to my favorite seaside chowder dive. I hate to think it's been a whole year since I've been here. But the seagulls still seem to be happy to see me, as I am to be with them again. This is my happy place, and I love myself for bringing me here today, for leaving the laundry undone and the grass unmowed. Who cares? I am here."

Or in the park, "Sitting here alone, with just a few birds for company, I am realizing how tired I am. I'm so tired I could cry. In fact, I think I'm too tired to cry. Even crying would be too much effort. Will I ever feel rested enough?"

Who am I writing to? What is the purpose of this writing? I almost always begin by describing where I am, capturing the scene, recording wherever I happen to be, in regard to what I'm doing or trying to get done. This is a good technique for focusing on the present, like a verbal meditation. Inevitably, the words evolve into how I feel about whatever is happening and what my thoughts are, and then, I just let it run wild. Sometimes, I say things that surprise me. A truth will come out that I hadn't fully realized until the words are formed.

I never thought about the process before I started writing this chapter. But as I wrote about the journaling practice, I tried to reconstruct how I use it. I actually had to walk away from the laptop, where I was sitting at the table in my hideaway cabin up north. I walked outside and found a sunny spot, where a big tree blocked the wind as it sweeps up from the cliff above the ocean. I sat on the grass in the sun, enjoying its warmth. Once I found the right spot, I started writing in the journal. I began by describing my surroundings and what was most pressing on my mind. I realized this is almost always how I begin.

You see, having done this for years without thinking much about it, I had to consciously watch my process so I could describe it to you. I recommend beginning your journal practice this way because it grounds you. It helps you focus on the present moment, and then, exactly what you need to say in that moment will come out.

Since I'm not good at doing traditional meditation, such as sitting still with my eyes closed, mentally repeating a mantra, or counting my breaths, I find this method works better. I have tried at least a dozen different types of meditation. They always feel like work, like I have to force myself to do it. I know so many people for whom this is terribly important and who rave about it, so I have pushed myself to keep trying different ways to meditate, but that style just doesn't suit me.

Writing, however, is the perfect way for me to be present. Using words, I find my center. Through written expression, I am able to release the pus along with the infected thoughts, cleaning out the wounds that inevitably reveal themselves.

If you are someone who is a deep thinker, with more to say than there are people to say it to, then this is very likely a practice you will love.

Exercises for a Journal Practice

- Buy a blank journal. Bookstores and stationery stores usually have blank journals for sale.

- Decide on a time of day you would be comfortable pouring your thoughts into a journal. It could be first thing in the morning, at the end of the day, or as a break between a couple of your activities. Decide when a good time would be to sit down, be alone with your thoughts, and write. This is the way to make it a regular practice.

- Make a list of places that would be ideal for journal writing. It could be a coffee shop, a park, a café, or someplace at your home.

- You don't have to write in the journal every day. That does work for many people, as it gets a rhythm and a habit started. Try to write in your journal at least once a week. Notice how writing in your journal affects your life and your state of mind. Write about it.

CHAPTER 6

Step 3. Rest: Time to Recharge

Zoom! This is how we go through each day in the American culture. For most of us, from the moment we wake up, straight until evening, it's a balancing act to get through everything our day requires. As I said in an earlier chapter, no matter how much we have already accomplished, there is always pressure to do more. This amounts to long to-do lists and booking up every minute of our time. It results in a culture of people who are frequently exhausted. Even days that are technically off tend to be catch-up days, where household and family errands fill up that time. If we are lucky, we are able to squeeze in some socializing, but it's rare that we take time to just do nothing at all so we can fully rest and recharge. I cannot tell you how much my soul craves time to do nothing.

To Do Nothing Is a Powerful Act

Do you crave rest? Do you find yourself looking ahead, wondering when you will be done with whatever you are doing and have some blank space to just stop and breathe quietly for a while? Rest is something we don't get enough of. There is always so much pressure to do things, whether it's related to our job, our family, or social activities. But sometimes, what we deeply need is some space to do nothing at all.

I started looking for ways to incorporate doing nothing into my day as a way of slowing down and being present, rather than constantly focusing on the future. It's not easy at first, when you are in the habit of pushing to complete the to-do list, but I found that once I started, I craved these breaks. The simplest one is to find a place to be still for five minutes, in between tasks. For instance, after I've finished massaging a client or two, I take a five-minute break to sit, breathe, and relax. When I come home from the grocery store, after I've put all the food away, I spend a little time just being quiet for a bit before going on to the next task. It is a guilty pleasure, although I'm feeling less and less guilty about it.

In fact, I now seek out interesting places that lend themselves to relaxing. You may be thinking journaling performs this function, but even that is still doing something. It's helpful. It's therapeutic. But it's still an activity. This practice is about finding the best places to do absolutely nothing. I notice inviting spots around my city, where public benches have been placed, and I choose ones that are in appealing locations or have a nice view. It's fun to spend a few minutes people-watching or close my eyes and let my rhythm slow down. Sometimes, I set the timer on my phone for five minutes of rest, so I can shut my eyes and just let go, and I am always struck by how long five minutes seems when I am doing nothing at all.

There are many ways to put downtime into your schedule and a variety of ways you can rest. On workdays, take a walk during your lunch break and get away from it all. If your job allows, take a short recess, and go someplace restorative. For a while, I worked in hospitals and found they had gardens or ponds that were lovely places to regroup.

In addition to tiny rest periods throughout your day, it's good to have a big chunk of time where there is nothing on your calendar. No work, no dates with friends, no errands, no projects. Do you ever have days like that? Whether you can manage a full day to yourself weekly, monthly, or even a couple of days a year, it's important to have time where you can fully let go. It's necessary to occasionally unplug from activity in order to regroup and recharge.

Find the Right Place for Your Break

Learning the best places to recharge becomes a survival strategy. And it can also be a fun exploration. If you like to take walks, choose a route where you can stop and rest for a little while. Perhaps there is a path through a park or someplace where there are public benches where you can sit for a few minutes. In downtown areas, there are public squares and places that surround buildings that are designed for people to stop and linger. Look for the ones with fountains and lots of foliage.

If you live near a beach, find a spot in the sand where you can spread out a blanket and listen to the waves while your mind slows down. The sound and rhythm of the ocean is incredibly soothing. It can act like a tranquilizer, calming down your breathing and your thoughts and washing away stress.

In areas with forests, seek out a place under a tree where you can lie down and look up at the sky through the leaves. It's beautiful to observe the pattern of the leaves with the blue backdrop of the sky. There's something very restorative about stretching out under a tree. It's blissfully meditative to lie there quietly. The older the tree, the more tranquil it is. If you live in a city, perhaps there is a park where you can sit or lie down and remain undisturbed for a while. It's fun to search for special places just for this purpose.

Lakes and ponds are good for short escapes. There's something very soothing about water, whether it's the ocean, a river, or a lake. Most cities have someplace like this in a public park.

Other places you can rest might be found at home. If you have a porch, a balcony, or a patio, you can put a lounge chair there where you can rest quietly, read, or just close your eyes. If you have a backyard, you can set up a resting spot there or try putting up a hammock. Whenever I lie in a hammock, even if I start off with a book to read, I don't get very far before I close the book, along with my eyes, and just drift. There's something about the gentle rocking that lends itself to this.

On my front porch, I have a chaise lounge with a thick, dark green cushion. I often take these breaks, stretching out and enjoying brief naps. The porch is surrounded by a tall, lush flower garden, and sitting there immediately makes me feel good. Being outdoors helps me relax. It's a beautiful, peaceful place. After being still for a short while, I feel so rested, I arise juiced with fresh energy. This greatly reinforces what a difference even a brief break can make. I do have to keep my eyes closed at these times, because if I look at the garden, I will start to notice a weed that needs to be plucked or a shrub that needs pruning, and I'll get pulled back into being busy. But that's just me.

When the Weather Isn't Suited for Going Outdoors

Some of the activities I mentioned only work when the weather is nice. In the winter or on cold or rainy days, there are plenty of ways to relax indoors.

Inside your house or apartment, create a place to lie down and rest. Even if it's just part of a room, divided by a folding screen, place some cushions or a recliner there, and make a place that's designed for your break. If you have a meditation practice, then you probably already have a place like this and are resting during meditation. If meditation doesn't suit you, spend this time listening to music or a guided visualization recording, or just close your eyes and bask in the stillness of doing nothing. If you live with other people and it's impossible to find a quiet spot at home, go to the library. They are nice, quiet places, and it's easy to find a comfortable seat, out of the way, where you can close your eyes and either relax in silence, or use earbuds to listen to some peaceful music or a guided relaxation recording.

If you have a fireplace, building a fire and watching the flames is very hypnotic. This can be combined with slow music in the background, creating an atmosphere of bliss.

Taking a hot bath is another way to rest and do nothing. It especially feels like a treat when you take one during the day, when you would otherwise be engaged in an activity. This is one of my favorites. I have a set of votive candles on the bathroom shelf I pull out and an inflatable bathtub pillow suction cupped to the back of the tub. I usually take a hot bath one night a week. Occasionally, I take one during the day, often during the winter months, which feels especially decadent.

You can make a restful spot by using large pieces of fabric to curtain off the corner of a room, making a special tent where you can disappear. Use this as your resting spot. It's fun to use your creativity to make a special place for yourself.

If Your Home Is Not a Restful Place

It's easier to do this at home if you live alone or have times when there's no one else there. If this is not the case, and it's hard to find quiet time at home, look for places in your community that can be your refuge. There are health clubs and spiritual centers that have meditation rooms for members. Search out quiet places in your community. Certain restaurants or cafés have very quiet atmospheres. Museums are also good places where you can find a quiet spot in front of a work of art and just rest. Perhaps the next time you have a free afternoon, you can explore places in your surroundings with this in mind. Bookstores, botanical gardens, art galleries, nurseries all have places where you can sit and have a period of quiet rest.

If you live with other people, and there's always activity in your home, taking yourself out to a movie during the day can serve as a great escape, as can going out to lunch at a quiet, upscale restaurant.

The purpose of this is to give you some room to stop doing. Depending on where you live and what your life is like, it could be more challenging to find places to retreat to. But they are there. You just have to find or create them.

Watching TV at night may feel like your rest time, and for many people, that's the only time they stop being active. However, it makes a big difference to take some time to slow down during the day, to have at least one day a week, or even part of a day, where you are not busy. It's more restorative than collapsing on the couch at the end of a busy day.

Cultural Traditions of Rest

When I was in my twenties, I went on a long trip for several months to Southeast Asia. I happened to arrive in Bali the day before what they call "Quiet Day." On that day, everything on the island is shut down. No cars or buses run. No restaurants are open. No fires are lit. It's a day when the entire island hits the off switch. All food has been prepared in advance because no cooking is done. A local person explained to me they do this so malevolent spirits will think everyone has left the island, and they will move on. I thought it was wonderful this whole culture observed a day when absolutely everything and everyone came to a halt and rested.

Even the Bible talks about having a day of rest each week. Many spiritual traditions honor a day of rest. Clearly, there is something to this.

In Spain, businesses close for hours in the middle of the day so people can have a leisurely lunch and rest, known as a siesta. In Italy, a similar tradition is called the *riposo*. People go home and have a long, leisurely lunch, followed by a nap.

The middle of the afternoon is an ideal time to doze, as your body is digesting its midday meal. This is often the hour of the day when you feel groggy, and your natural biological clock is programmed to nap.

Think of it as a way to reboot. You know when you reboot things, they work better. As the deeply down-to-earth writer Anne Lamott says, "Almost everything will work again if you unplug it for a few minutes, including you."

How to Set Aside Time to Rest

The amount of time you rest can vary, anywhere from ten minutes of sitting still on a park bench to spending a whole afternoon at a public park. Take a look at the rhythm of your life, and see where you can fit it in. Like anything, once it starts to become part of your routine, you do it regularly.

Taking some time to rest on your lunch break during the workday can go a long way toward recharging you before returning to your job. Small daily rests are fantastic. Combined with a longer rest period during the week, this will make a big difference in your energy level as well as your general emotional mood. One of my friends refers to this kind of day off as a soul retreat. Get out of town for the day, and go exploring, either someplace you haven't been or a favorite place you love to go. Getting out of our familiar routine helps us change mental patterns as well as relieves stress. This is when we often have important insights or new ideas about our lives.

If you have children, see if someone can watch them for an hour or two once a week so you have some time to yourself. If you don't have a partner who can do it and a sitter is too expensive, find another parent you can trade with so you each get some alone time.

Scheduling this time after completing something gives you motivation to get things done and provides a reward for doing them. Sometimes, it's hard to take a break when we have many pressing things to do. Getting some of those things completed helps you feel deserving of a reward. We often think of rewards as something material, such as buying ourselves a treat. We rarely think of giving ourselves some space as a reward, which is why it is all that more valuable.

It's so helpful to give yourself a chance to be still, to rest, to let go. Let the swirl of energy that is constantly driving you come to a halt. Taking time to stop and slow down gives you a chance to evaluate what you're doing and prioritize what's really important. It also helps recharge your batteries and strengthens your immune system.

Once you start enjoying the breathing space of rest, it won't be hard to find pockets of time to indulge yourself. You'll notice how good you feel when you are rested, relaxed, and calm.

Getting Good Sleep

Part of good self-care is making sure all the basics of health are being maintained. Resting during the day allows for natural rhythms of energy expenditure to recharge so you can feel your best. It's also important to get good sleep at night. Approximately 40 million Americans suffer from chronic sleep disorder, and about 20 million have occasional sleep problems. Having a good night's sleep is the foundation for feeling rested. The naps and breaks I described above are not meant to be a remedy for lack of sleep at night.

There are a number of reasons people don't sleep well. The body and mind need to be physically and mentally prepared for sleep. Technology keeps us engaged constantly with smart phones, tablets, and social media. In order to sleep well, we need to unplug from this stimulation and wind down at night, turning off all those things that capture our attention so we can go inward. Situations we are struggling with can keep us up worrying, going through mental loops. This is not productive, but it can become habitual.

Training your body and mind to sleep well involves creating new habits. Here are a few tips to use so you can get a good night's sleep.

About an hour before you want to sleep, begin your wind-down routine. Disengage from stimuli. Turn off the TV; close the laptop, phone, or tablet; and settle into bed. It is best to do activities that slow you down and don't engage you. That's why watching TV is generally not best right before bed, but that depends on what programs you watch. If you watch something soothing, that might work for you. Drama and violence are not good choices to watch right before going to bed. The same goes for reading. Some books will help you fall asleep, whereas a page-turner can keep you up half the night. Choose something that will help slow down your mind. Sometimes, I read right before sleep. I choose books that are interesting but not so engaging they require a lot of mental energy or trigger my emotions. It's helpful to have something that takes your mind off your everyday life, so you aren't lying in bed thinking of the problems you need to solve or worrying about the ones you aren't sure about.

Adult coloring books are a good way to wind down. They are just engaging enough to keep you from slipping into a mental loop, but sufficiently soothing so you can quiet your mind.

I got into a routine of playing a rather mindless pattern-matching game on my phone. I began doing it to get myself away from looking at social media at night. After a while, my whole body became habituated to the routine. I knew when I started playing the game, it meant I would soon be going to sleep, so I naturally became more and more sleepy as I played. It became part of my new sleep routine. If you do something like this on an electronic device like a phone or tablet, implement a blue light filter that will change the quality of the light it puts out in the evening hours, so the light from the device doesn't keep you from winding down.

It is helpful to stop eating at least three hours before you go to bed. Eating a large meal late at night does not lend itself to restfulness. If you are hungry, eat a piece of fruit or have some hot milk or a piece of toast.

In extreme cases, medication can be used, but sleep drugs are often habit forming and disrupt your body's natural ability to go through the process slowing down to sleep. These should be used only in extreme cases. Save them for when you have something specific keeping you awake, such as something stressful you have to do the following day or a serious problem causing you anxiety and keeping you from being able to wind down. Don't rely on medications for sleep; instead, train your body to sleep on its own.

Training Your Mind to Unwind

Although it may not seem that way at times, you do have control over what you think. You can choose to put your mind in a tranquil place by purposely directing your thoughts when you finally close your eyes, in preparation for drifting off.

One way to begin this mental transition is to think of five things you are grateful for. Go through the things in your life that are good. Picture the people, the place you live, opportunities you have, and anything you consider positive. There are so many good things you automatically take for granted, but if you think about it, you're really lucky to have these positive things in your life. Try this practice for a few weeks, choosing five gratitudes. It can be simple things. For example, "I am grateful I have a protected place to live. I am grateful for the way the soft, comfortable sheets feel against my skin. I am grateful for my sweet, affectionate dogs. I am grateful to have good neighbors. I am grateful folks liked what I made for dinner." There, that's five. There are many, many things to be grateful for.

Gratitude stimulates the reward center in the brain and gives you a sense of pleasure and peace. This increases the production of serotonin, which helps balance your mood and makes you feel good.

If there is a problem that keeps getting in the way of turning off your thoughts, whether it is a world problem or a personal one, imagine the ideal outcome. Imagine the problem resolved. Picturing the best possible solution will help you relax. Since there isn't anything practical you can do about it while you're lying in bed, visualizing the ideal result and focusing on that will help you feel peace.

Picture places where you have positive memories. Perhaps there is a place you've vacationed or somewhere you would call your happy place. Guide your imagination to this place, and the good feelings you associate with it will help you relax and let go. By this time, you are already tired and ready for sleep; you just need to unplug your mind from being busy so you can let that drowsiness pull you deeper into the zone.

Once you get a nighttime routine down, you will find it easier and easier to go to sleep. Try to go to bed at the same time each night. Your body becomes accustomed to habits. This is a good one to nurture.

Getting good sleep and rest is essential for overall well-being. This will help you feel your best and thus be ready for whatever comes up in your life.

Exercises for Getting Rest

- Choose a way to incorporate a five-minute rest break every day, whether it's part of your workday or otherwise. Find a place where you can sit quietly with your eyes closed for five minutes.

- Arrange to take a twenty-minute power nap several times a week. Set a timer on your phone, close your eyes, and let all the energy slow down.

- Unplug from everything at least once a week, either for the entire day or a few hours. No social media or news. Focus on the moment, in the present.

CHAPTER 7

Step 4. Nourishment: A Hedonist's Guide to Healthy Eating

Are you hungry? What sounds good?

Feeding ourselves well is an essential part of self-care. How could it not be? Eating is primal among our most basic needs.

Working in the field of spas and relaxation, one might consider me a pleasure-seeking hedonist. Therefore, my relationship to food is all about pleasure. Well, pleasure and health. Part of what makes me enjoy certain foods is knowing they are made of healthy ingredients that are enhancing my physical well-being. I love foods that are rich with the vibrant colors of fresh fruits and vegetables, delectable textures, and rich flavors. And they provide a high level of nutrients.

Meals should not be rushed, quickly scarfed pieces of processed, packaged food products. Companies make a lot of money selling these products, as well as fast food, and spend a lot of money advertising them to convince people to eat the packaged and mass-produced products rather than fresh, delectable food.

Since our bodies are basically made from the elements in our food, it's very important to eat foods that are highly nutritious. Fruits, vegetables, beans, legumes, nuts, seeds, dairy products, whole grains, unprocessed meats, fish, and herbs all have lots of beneficial nutrients. Unfortunately, highly processed food and fast food have become a large part of the American diet, to the point where this is what many people crave. However, eating a diet that is high in white flour, white rice, fat, sugar, salt, and chemical additives can contribute to serious diseases over a period of time.

As an alternative health practitioner, I am wary of all the things that are part of normal life that contribute to disease. I think about everything from toxic thoughts to highly processed food and the impact they have on our health. With eating, I recommend following the 80/20 rule, where you eat 80 percent pure, whole foods and 20 percent treats that might have white flour or sugar. Thus, you can occasionally have a sugary snack or order something in a restaurant where you don't know all the ingredients, knowing the majority of the food you eat is healthy, so a rare splurge is okay. One meal isn't going to make you sick or healthy. It takes time for food to have an effect on you one way or another.

Everything you eat, if possible, should consist of foods you love. That way, you are feeding more than your stomach. You are providing a feast for all of your senses. Choose foods that have bright colors and are artistically presented, with fresh, rich, intense flavors.

Here are some tips for making your meals as restorative as possible:

Your favorite foods will likely be different from mine, so as I describe the way I play with these concepts, know you will create your own way of eating mindfully and joyfully, but the main thing I want you to take away from this is about quality, not quantity.

My very favorite foods are fruits. Mangos, mandarins, crisp apples, and berries grace my meals every day. I love foods that look beautiful, taste divine, and feel like they are benefiting my health with every chew and swallow.

When you look at the classic foods around the world, much of the exotic appeal comes from the beautiful array of fruits, vegetables, meats, seafood, and sauces that incorporate flavorful herbs and spices. The best foods are prepared fresh. They are not heavily processed and packaged for convenience. In Europe, they have traditions of leisurely meals, where people spend hours slowly enjoying each dish, taking their time to savor the food and the entire experience of eating.

Whether you like to spend time cooking and following elaborate recipes or simply assembling plates of combinations that go well together, you can make your own culinary experience deeply pleasurable, without it costing a lot of money or taking a lot of time. It's really a matter of prioritizing the experience.

You can arrange fruits and vegetables so your plate looks like a work of art, making it all the more appetizing. Garnishes of nuts, seeds, and herbs make the food tastier and more appetizing. Play around with using different plates and platters to present your food in order to treat yourself at home as though you were in a high-end restaurant. This is another form of self-care.

When I was in Italy, a country well known for its epicurean delights, I was struck by how simple and delicious much of the food preparation was. Vegetables were grilled or pan-fried and embellished with a drizzle of olive oil, a squeeze of lemon, some chopped garlic, and that's it. Simple and delicious. Play with garnishes. That's what students learn in culinary academies: the art of garnishing. It's fun, it's creative, it's tasty, and you can make healthy food very appetizing that way. Take some broccoli, steam it, drizzle with olive oil that has had some garlic sautéed in it, and then decorate it with a tablespoon of chopped, toasted walnuts. Yum.

Experiment.

Try different fresh herbs as a garnish. Some chopped fresh basil, perhaps, or parsley. Or try grating some fresh lemon or orange zest. I have a lemon tree and became quite an aficionado of zesting and began collecting a variety of zesters. It really adds great flavor, texture, and color to all sorts of dishes. And it is chocked full of powerful antioxidants, the substance that fights cancer and disease in your body.

Making good food can be very easy. One of my favorite summer dinners is steamed vegetables topped with a poached egg and a sprinkle of fresh parmesan cheese. This is particularly good on asparagus, summer squash, broccoli, or green beans. As the egg yolk breaks and soaks into the vegetable, it is rather luxurious. I try to get the freshest eggs I can find, buying them at the farmer's market whenever possible. The green vegetables, topped by the egg, with its bright orange yolk, create a beautiful presentation. Get in the habit of treating yourself like an honored guest, creating food presentations like you would for company or that you might receive in a fine restaurant.

Preparing gorgeous, appetizing food is a form of self-love. It's nourishing way beyond nutrition. I know a lot of people who think if they don't have someone else to cook for, it's not worth bothering. Sometimes, they eat very poorly when they are by themselves. I'm talking about watching TV, while mindlessly gobbling potato chips, frozen pizza, or some quickly microwaved frozen dinner. Please, treat yourself better than this. If you make a dish that has three or four servings, you can freeze portions for a later date. I bought a set of glass meal-sized freezer containers just for this purpose and a label maker, so at a glance I can look in my freezer and see the options.

I started making super healthy, tasty muffins because they are great treats, especially for breakfast, and they are very easy to freeze. Thirty seconds in the microwave after taking them out of the freezer, and they are perfect. Since I'm obsessed with healthy ingredients, I find muffin recipes and then substitute a lot of the ingredients for healthier ones, keeping the proportions and basics so they'll turn out okay. For instance, I have a banana muffin recipe (because muffins are easier to freeze than banana bread), and I substituted half the flour with rolled oats that I ground into a powder in my food processor. I also substituted dark maple syrup for the sugar and unsweetened applesauce for the fat. I often add dark chocolate chips and walnuts. They still come out good, and they're not that different nutritionally from having a bowl of oatmeal for breakfast, topped with bananas, walnuts, and maple syrup.

I promise you, if you start caring for yourself the way you would treat a beloved guest, your life will change. For one thing, you will become a happier person if little pleasures become part of your daily life, no matter where you are, who you are with, or what you are doing. As you go about your day, think about how you can get the most pleasure out of the time you spend eating. If you are at home, use nice accessories to make your meal appetizing and beautiful. Set up a special place to eat with pretty plates and accessories. When I went to England one summer, I bought two souvenirs. One was a teabag caddy shaped like a teapot. I'm a big tea drinker, so I keep this on my kitchen table and use it every morning. The other was a small, decorated plate, the perfect size for a muffin or piece of toast. These simple dishes enrich my experience of having breakfast every day.

When I go out of town on a solo getaway, which is what I like to do in order to recharge and write, I want to keep my costs down, so I bring food with me to minimize the expense of eating out. I'll bring a ripe avocado and mash it with lemon juice, garlic powder, and sea salt, making a delicious guacamole. I then take a carrot and slice it into slivers for dipping. I may also cut up a red bell pepper and chop up some tomatoes. With a little cheese and crackers, it makes a beautiful, healthy meal I can put together in a hotel room, arranged artistically on a platter.

I pack fruit, graham crackers, peanut butter, and goat cheese for breakfast, and cups of instant hot soup that only require boiling water from an electric hot pot I bring with me. I add sliced green onions and chopped peanuts to garnish the Thai noodle soup that comes in one of those just-add-water cups, and voila: a tasty and beautiful meal. I carry a couple of plates and a nice bowl for my food so I can transfer everything to my pretty dishes. It's easy, delicious, and beautifully presented. And healthy, as well. Most importantly, eating this way, with care to presentation and quality, simple ingredients, makes me feel incredibly well cared for. What are your favorite foods? What are some creative ways you can present them that can turn your meals into culinary delights? Which meal is your favorite one of the day?

What would your meals be like if every serving were, in some sense, a work of art? We see pictures of food in magazines, on websites, in TV commercials, in restaurant ads, foods that have been carefully arranged by a food stylist to make them appear appetizing. What if you did that for yourself, every time you ate?

You don't need a lot of money to live well. You just need to approach your life like it is a work of art, and you are an honored guest. Food is a pleasure you can use to treat yourself multiple times throughout the day, every day.

This is a way to care for yourself physically and emotionally; it can become a habit of delicious creativity.

Nourishment Exercises

- Start a recipe folder, where you can collect recipes of the foods you love to make and eat over and over again. You can print it out or keep it on your computer. I have a series of folders within a folder, with the foods and meals divided into categories.
- Make a list of your favorite foods and foods you want to incorporate into your diet more often.
- Buy a new cookbook or two.
- Discover some websites that have recipes for the kind of foods you like to eat, and visit them frequently to get good ideas. Add the winning recipes to your food folder.
- If you don't like to cook, make a list of prepared foods you find enhance your sense of well-being.

CHAPTER 8

Step 5. Mindful Money Management, or the Zen of Budgeting

Taking care of yourself so you are not stressing about money is the ultimate in self-care. It is number one in Abraham Maslow's hierarchy of needs: survival. Creative art expression, indulgences, rest: These are all secondary to making sure your basic needs for financial security are met.

Interestingly, this has very little to do with how much money you make.

You can be a millionaire and still be broke because you bought too many cars, houses, or tropical islands. Or you could be an average person accumulating a slew of credit cards in lieu of actual cash, in order to fund the things you want. On the other hand, you could have a small income, but with clever planning and practices, you could live quite comfortably on a shoestring.

It really doesn't matter how much you have, but how you go about allocating it.

This principle is especially important because many people hate to think about it. I have known people in every economic bracket who don't want to take a realistic look at their finances. Here are some strategies for living well on a minimal amount that I have developed over a lifetime of living well on a sporadic income.

Live beneath Your Means

The secret to mindful money management in one sentence is to live beneath your means. If you make $1,000, sock away $200 and live on $800. If you make $3,000, sock away $500. Or whatever you're able to do. And so on.

Since I have been self-employed most of my life, I have never felt sure about how much money I could count on. Not having a set salary, I never felt I had the luxury of accumulating debt because I couldn't be sure of being able to pay it back. So rather than rely on credit cards and loans, I have mainly lived on a cash basis.

When I arrived in California on my own, at the age of seventeen, right after graduating high school, I found bits of work here and there doing odd jobs. It was always possible to find something I could get paid for, but since I didn't have many skills at that age, these were all jobs for low pay. Therefore, I had to be creative from the very beginning. I was so excited to be out on my own, and moving from Pennsylvania to the

Northern California Bay Area in the 1970s was like a dream. I knew practically nothing about life, but I was going to make this work.

For a while, I lived in a chicken coop converted into a living space someone was renting on their rural property. It was very inexpensive, and having that place felt like a miracle, even though in many ways, it was quite primitive. I didn't care. I was happy having a place all to myself. Another place I lived was a tiny cottage in the countryside that was old and falling apart, but the rent was very low. There were several similar structures on the property, and a lively group of people lived there, so it was fun, even though the buildings were crumbling. We made the place into a tiny community, which always had something entertaining going on, and it was very affordable to live there. There are always free or low-cost ways to acquire goods and ways to have fun. There are free concerts, buy-nothing groups, where things are given away for free, and other ways to get things without spending money. Freecycle.org is a website you can sign up for according to your locality where people post things they have to give away and others post things they want. Facebook has a Buy Nothing group that is similar. After a while, searching for deals becomes habit.

During those early years of having very little when I got settled in California and the subsequent years of going to college and eventually becoming a massage therapist, I developed a mindset to stay within my budget. I did not go to college, by the way, to become a massage therapist. It just sort of happened. I was studying psychology and planned to be a psychotherapist, but I got interested in massage when a friend and fellow student became a massage therapist and practiced on me. I thought the bodywork was so profound and healing in a multitude of nonverbal ways, and that was what my soul really wanted to do. So rather than follow the path of academia, I followed my heart. I went to massage school while I was still at university, and by the time I got my bachelor's degree, I had a thriving private practice going. But the income was unstable. Some days, I saw five clients; other days, two or none. I loved the work and knew this was right for me, but I had to be careful about money. And that's when I developed the mindset of living simply.

I call it a mindset because it has a lot more to do with a way of thinking than looking at numbers. I enjoyed looking for free or low-cost ways of doing everything. I shopped at flea markets and yard sales, went to clothing swaps, and found out about free entertainment. When possible, I traded massage for goods and services I needed. There are always free or low-cost ways of doing things in college towns, and even after I graduated, I stuck around. As the years passed and I became more stable financially, I still tried to live as cheaply as possible. That meant I was often spending less than I needed to, so I had savings that accumulated if I wanted to do something special like go on a trip.

The mentality of knowing how to live inexpensively stuck with me. It made me feel secure. That savings account was my security blanket. Living cheaply became almost a game, to see how inexpensively I could live, and my savings account was my treasure. My lifestyle did not require me to wear fashionable clothes or have costly accessories. And I liked it that way.

When Money Becomes a Problem

Years later, when I was married and life had become more complicated, I had a day where there were a couple hundred dollars left in my checking account that had to last me for two weeks before I got paid. Our basic bills were covered. We just needed groceries and gas, and I figured we'd be okay. I went to the market and spent $150 on food for the household, filled up my tank, and assumed we'd be fine. Then a friend texted who wanted to get together for lunch. Yeah, I could squeeze that in, but then that was it. No more dates until I got paid. Everything was going seamlessly until our dog started vomiting and displaying big signs of discomfort, and I had to rush him to the vet. I wasn't thinking about cost at that point, just hoping the vet could figure out what was wrong with him. Oh, and very grateful to have a credit card for the vet bill, which exceeded our savings.

But I didn't say a prayer of gratitude. The credit card was something I took for granted. It was my safety net, and it came in handy in an emergency. I'd worry about paying it off later. And I did. Making payments on the card became a priority until the balance was back to zero.

This is a common scenario. Our basic expenses are in our budget, but then things come up. Friends want us to do something that costs money, the car breaks down, something else breaks, or our child needs something from us: money, money, money.

Worrying about money is stressful. I want to help you handle finances in such a way that you don't have to worry about it.

Creating the Stash Habit

In principle, it's simple. Spend less than you earn, and have a savings account for emergencies. But in reality, it's much more complicated. There are so many factors that affect our finances.

One could also say the way to maintain a healthy weight is to eat the number of calories you are likely to burn in a day. Just stick to the calorie count. Simple, right?

But similar to eating food, spending money involves very complicated behaviors. It can be emotional. We spend money to buy things and do things that make us happy, make us feel like we fit in, help us keep up with our friends. And just like one might analyze what and why one eats certain foods and in certain quantities, the same can be true of spending money. In both cases, a certain amount is necessary. But there are situations where we can lose control and where we spend a lot for emotional reasons. Then emergencies and unexpected situations come up that blindside us.

Again, like eating food, spending money is often something we don't track. It's all very well to tell people how many calories they should limit themselves to or how much to budget for this or that, but most of us don't grow up with a habit of tracking and measuring everything. Most people are not self-trained accountants with spreadsheets listing all of their expenditures.

I was having lunch with a friend one day and paid for my lunch with my ATM card. After getting my receipt, I pulled out my checkbook and deducted the amount, since I needed to keep track of the accurate balance in my checking account. My friend was very surprised that I was tracking my expenses. I asked her how she otherwise knew how much she was spending. She shrugged.

I feel strongly that part of our basic education, along with reading, math, science, and history, should be how to manage money. But they don't teach us this. In some households, parents train their kids about money management. They give them an allowance or pay them to do chores. Children learn they only have a certain amount, and that's all they can spend on treats and toys and whatever it is they want. But many parents do not teach their children this. Many of them are struggling themselves with debt and financial shortfalls.

I've talked with a lot of people about this. Many people I know have money problems. They try to ignore it, hoping a miracle will happen, that maybe some relative they've forgotten about will leave them something in their will or something else will occur and make the problem go away. For some people, this may be the most important chapter in this book. I take this very seriously. And I have fun coming up with creative ways to live well inexpensively. Maybe my next book will be called *Living Well on a Shoestring*.

My parents were careful with money and taught me to be. They gave me an allowance. I made extra money babysitting. When I was still in grammar school, I got a minimum-wage job at the library, restocking returned books. My parents taught me how to budget, and it was a behavior that became automatic, like doing my homework and tidying up my room. Just part of life.

But as I got older, friends confided to me about their financial problems, and many asked for my help. When I was in my twenties, I had a friend who asked me to look over her finances and help her because she had more debt than she could pay off. I sat down with her and saw her paycheck was mostly eaten up by her rent, car payment, and food, and everything else went on credit cards. She was so stretched, she couldn't even make the minimum payment on her cards. After going over her numbers, I came to the conclusion the only thing she could do was file bankruptcy and get a fresh start. This was not what she wanted to hear, but she had waited until things were way out of control before asking for help.

Like much of this book, I'm going to swerve away from the norms and pressures we often experience, that cause us to live in a way that makes us end up feeling overwhelmed and stressed. In American culture, it's hard to stay out of debt. In order to live the way we want, do the things we enjoy, have the things that make life beautiful, pleasurable, and interesting, we often spend a lot more money than we have. Advertisements encourage us to live this way, with payment plans for everything. I'm sure you know what I'm talking about. It's pretty hard to grow up in this country without being exposed to this.

This isn't about judgment. I understand we all look at money and spending habits differently. I am bringing this up because this is absolutely essential to taking good care of yourself. It's also an area that is taboo to talk about. It's easier to talk about a difficult relationship than to discuss money problems. There's a lot of shame assigned to financial difficulties, so people don't talk about it. And because we don't talk about it, we don't learn from each other, the way we learn about healthier food or how to navigate constantly changing technology. So we walk around with huge anxieties about making ends meet that we feel inclined to keep secret. It's horrible. That's why I consider this such an important chapter.

In order to get your finances in order, you have to develop new habits and new ways of thinking. For everything you spend money on, think about whether there's an alternative. I have known people with more debt than they could pay back who still went out to eat and spent money on unnecessary things and basically ignored the fact they were making their situation worse. This is very common.

The curious part of me likes making things, so that helps me limit my spending. I enjoy cooking. I've made many of my own clothes. I like learning how to use tools so I can repair things myself. The thing I like to splurge on are my road trips up the coast. Later, I will share some of my tricks in doing that inexpensively, as well.

Credit Is Not Money

Credit cards are easy to get. And this is the problem. So often, people see credit as a way of increasing their ability to spend and have a good time. I had one friend who had a credit card just for vacations. Whenever she wanted to go on a trip, she used that card. When living the way you want involves getting deeper in debt, you are fooling yourself if you pretend the credit is actually additional money. My friend was acting like she had a vacation account when she really was getting deeper in debt, because she didn't have the funds to pay it off when she came back from vacation.

I had another friend who pulled out credit cards when she ran out of cash, and after she had several that were fully maxed out, she was desperate to come up with some kind of consolidation plan, because she was reaching the point where she had too many payments to make, and monthly interest was in the hundreds of dollars. A consolidation plan is where all the debt gets pooled together into one amount, and instead of making several monthly payments on a multitude of cards, you just make one payment. The problem with this is that the balance is very high; these consolidation plans are usually very high interest. Often, once people reach this stage, the minimum payment is already pretty high, so people only pay the minimum; interest continues to accrue, and it takes forever to pay it off.

This happened with my friend. She had a habit of going out to happy hour after work every day. It was emotional. After work, she didn't want to go home to an empty house, so she went out where there were always a group of people chatting at the bar. She spent way more than she earned doing this.

Consolidating the loans didn't solve the problem because she could never pay the money off this way. She had to break the habit that was creating the problem. She was not learning the lesson because she was in the grip of a psychological need that was not going to go away by my explaining the logic. After talking about it with her, I learned her mom had very similar habits. She was raised by a single mom who loved her and wanted to treat her to things, so this credit card strategy had been modeled for her.

This is why it's important to look at what we learn from our families and our childhoods. Basic habits of how we live, how we eat, how we spend money come from modeling the behavior we observed growing up. Now, it doesn't have to be like this. Once we become aware of certain patterns and where they came from, we can change them. But until we take a look at how our families did things and how we followed those behaviors, we act automatically. If that's not working for us, we have to make changes. And we can.

Schools Should Teach Us Basic Money Management

As I stated earlier, since using money is as basic to our lives as breathing, this should be taught as part of our education. We need to learn how to make a budget, how to save up for big purchases, how to manage loans, and how to build wealth. We need to learn the strategies for saving, so we can buy houses and cars, as well as how to save for retirement and to have savings accounts for emergencies, to finance vacations, and to cover other big expenditures. We need these skills, but many people don't have them.

It may seem obvious that we need to make more than we spend, but with our current financial models, it is very easy to get into trouble with credit. Finance companies are making fortunes while we are losing our shirts. In American culture, we are encouraged to keep spending money, whether we have it or not. Our culture is built on advertisements that psychologically convince us that having or doing certain things will give us a better, happier life, and these cravings become so strong, they override common sense.

Thus, we have a financial system in our culture that encourages us to get into trouble. It's unhealthy, just like eating trans fats or way too much sugar.

The advantage of the bankruptcy system is, it allows you to get rid of your debt and have a fresh start. But if you don't learn the lesson of financial management, you could end up filing for bankruptcy over and over again and ruining your credit.

I realize my approach to money and spending is different from many people, and that's one reason I'm writing this, as I think I have some good ideas to share. It's important to understand that having fun doesn't have to be expensive. Although I have enjoyed extravagant things, like foreign travel and elegant meals, I also have spent quite a bit of my life living simply and still managed to have a good time. But even with travel, I have been mindful. In my twenties, I traveled around the world for almost two years and only spent about $20k the whole time. I traveled through Southeast Asia, where it was cheap, and I learned how to do it by spending hardly any money. I was a big fan of the book *Southeast Asia on a Shoestring*, from the Lonely Planet group; it had lots of tips on where to stay, eat, and have fun for budget travelers. In this chapter, I will share my tips and techniques. But the most important thing to remember is, your sanity and security are number one. Nothing is more important than taking care of yourself on the most primal level.

The thing about credit cards is this: Let's say there's a piece of furniture you want to buy for your home that costs $3,000. Either you save up money for a few months or a year until you have $3,000 and then go out and pay for the furniture in full, or you put it on a credit card and make payments afterwards until it's paid off. Either way, you must come up with $3,000, whether you accumulate it in advance or pay for it after purchasing. If you pay for it afterwards, you are paying the $3,000, plus the interest that accrues. Sometimes, it's worth it to pay more so you can have the item sooner. If you choose to do it this way, make a plan so you know when you're going to have your loan paid off.

If you find this is a difficult topic for you to focus on, you are not alone. Our economic and social structure is always trying to pull more from us than we have. It can really be overwhelming, when you are building a family or setting up your life and trying to have everything it takes to live comfortably in our world.

Being Creative with Mindful Money Management

Have some fun with this. There are many ways to live well without spending a lot.

The basic idea is to figure out how to live frugally in some areas so you have money to splurge in other areas. An awful lot of spending is done mindlessly on things that are not really worth it, especially when it comes to small expenses. We often don't think about whether we really need to buy things; we just do it. And the small things add up. Just one example is picking up lunch to take to work instead of making something at home to bring in with you. Maybe you spend $10 to $12 each day to get a sandwich or some takeout. That's $50 to $60 per week, or $200 to $240 per month. In six months, that becomes $1,200 to $1,400. That could cover the cost of a nice weekend getaway. Or it could be sitting in your savings account when your car breaks down. And if all it takes is getting a loaf of bread and some lunch meat, it's a very easy way to save money without much sacrifice. This is just one simple example, but there are oodles of opportunities like this, where you can make a difference that really adds up.

Do you have a dollar amount where if something is under that amount, you don't give it much thought? $5? $10? $20? I look at every expenditure, no matter how small, and I ask myself, do I need this? Is this worth it? Is there something better I could do with this money?

Make a List of Priorities

A good way to get started is to make a list of splurges you don't want to sacrifice. What are the special treats you want to do, whether you have the money or not? In other words, what are the things you would pull out a credit card for? There's no judgment. You deserve to do and have the things that make you happy. But be mindful. Clarify what they are, how much they cost, and how often you want to do them. Figure out how much money you need to have each month to cover these things. Even if one of those things is to go on a cruise once a year, how much do you need to set aside towards that every month? No, you can't just pull out the cruise credit card. We're not doing that anymore.

Once you have identified your list of extras, look at your weekly spending patterns, and figure out what you can give up in order to have a few bucks to set aside for those things, and put the money in a special, designated account. For instance, if there's a performance you want to go to and a ticket costs $60, what can you forgo in order to have that money? What things do you spend money on that you could give up without missing too much? As you list the things you really want money for, make another list of things you wouldn't mind sacrificing. You're identifying your values. "I would much prefer to go see < fabulous musician > than to get Chinese takeout on Fridays." So instead of stopping by your favorite Chinese restaurant, pick up veggies and shrimp at the market, and go home and make a stir-fry. Then tuck the Chinese take-out money away for the concert.

One of my tricks is that I have several savings accounts. I have one account for property taxes, one for small expenses like vet bills, one for homeowner's insurance, one for big emergencies, like things that might break in the house or car repairs, and one for discretionary spending: my treats. Every time I get paid, I put some money in each of these accounts. I discovered Capital One 360, an online savings bank, not only pays higher interest than my local bank, but I could have different savings accounts I could label. I loved naming them. I named one of them "My Next Car" and started saving up for whenever I buy my next car. I figure I have to pay for the car one way or another, and I can either get a loan and pay for it after I acquire it and pay a lot of money in interest, or I can make the payments before I buy it, and buy it for a lower amount. Why not take the cheaper route? I have another account titled "Family Finances," where I put money to accrue for large purchases, home repairs, or any surprising expenses like medical bills, car repairs, and so on. Another account is named "Molly's Discretionary." That money mainly goes for trips I want to take or any large purchases.

Some people prefer to use a spreadsheet to categorize the different expenditures rather than have a lot of different accounts. Either way, it's a method to help you track what you're doing.

Housing

This is very likely your biggest expense. I suggest making a plan that will enable you to own your own home at some point. If you can scrape together a down payment, the best thing to do is purchase a home because then the monthly payment will not go up, and eventually you'll pay it off. It helps a lot with the cost if you can share a home with one or two other people. If that can work with your lifestyle, it makes paying for housing much more affordable. Whether you have a live-in partner or live with a friend or two, sharing the monthly payment makes a big difference. If you highly value your privacy and prioritize your alone time, see if there is any creative way to incorporate another person and still maintain strong boundaries, by organizing the space in such a way that you can have separate living spaces within the parameters of the property. Even if you share your home for just the first few years, it can help you enormously.

When we bought our house, I was in my thirties. At that time, it was possible to purchase a home with 10 percent down. In order to save up that down payment, I stopped all discretionary spending for two years. We only spent money on rent, gas, and food staples. My husband loved going out to lunch with his coworkers, but for two years, I made him bring lunches I made to take into work. We didn't go out. If we got together with friends, I cooked dinner rather than go to a restaurant to eat. It was tough, but we scraped it together. We weren't able to buy a home in the area we thought was the coolest place to live because it was too expensive. We had to get serious about facing our limitations and managed to find a good house in a decent neighborhood that wasn't my first choice, but that I eventually grew to love. You see, I knew rents would always go up. I knew the only way to have long-term financial stability was to buy. We did not have family who could give us a down payment, so we had to figure it out ourselves. But years later, we paid it off, and a huge pressure was off our backs.

I recommend living with other people, whether you have a partner or not. It really helps to have other people contributing. There are many ways to have your privacy. If you are able to get a down payment together to buy something, do it. If you are single, having housemates can help you make the mortgage payment. Find a home to buy in a decent location, knowing that everything else can be changed. You can get deals on homes that have problems, but many problems can be fixed. The temporary inconvenience is worth it in the long run.

Food

Eating is one of life's great pleasures, and it plays a big role in self-care. In fact, I've dedicated an entire chapter to food and nourishment. There is such a wide range of ways to eat, from having gardens where we grow most of our fruits and vegetables and raising chickens for fresh eggs all the way to having an array of favorite restaurants and cafés for our meals. How we choose to eat also plays a huge part in how we manage our money. I treat eating the same way I handle everything else. I make most of my own food from scratch, stocking up on staples and basic ingredients, which is pretty inexpensive, and then occasionally splurging on a nice meal at a favorite restaurant. When I was in high school, I became interested in healthy food and was a vegetarian for many years. I became fascinated with cooking, baking bread, and learning how to make all sorts of foods from scratch. This was another opportunity to be creative and experimental. I played around a lot. Some experiments didn't work out at all. I made lots of mistakes and learned a lot, and those early years of experimental cooking really stuck with me. I love playing around with food and discovering new dishes.

I got to the point where I hardly ever follow recipes. I often will begin with a recipe, then I begin substituting half the ingredients for other things I want to try, just to see how it will come out. Sometimes it works. Sometimes it doesn't. But it's really fun to experiment. I have learned not to be too experimental when having people over, if I don't know how well a dish will actually work.

One way to save on both costs and time is making large quantities of foods and then freezing them. My husband and housemate like quick meals they can microwave in five minutes or less. Whereas I will plan ahead and think up dishes that will use up leftovers or seasonal vegetables, they don't want to think about food at all until they are ravenously hungry and then want something they can eat right away.

A microwavable frozen meal you buy costs about 4 to 5 times what you would spend if you made the food from scratch. They are easy and convenient, cheaper than getting restaurant takeout, but still costly and often not the healthiest way to eat. Thus, I've gotten in the habit of making large quantities of household favorites like chicken parmesan, gourmet mac 'n' cheese, Pad Thai, and a number of other specialties I prepare in batches that make about ten servings at a time. I invested in some rectangular 3-cup glass Pyrex containers that are about the size of a standard frozen dinner, and when I make an elaborate dish, I make enough to fill up several of these single-serve meals. I even bought a label maker to put nice labels on them so they are easy to see and grab in the freezer. This has reduced our food costs considerably and makes it very easy to eat well, for minimal cost. This is especially good if you live alone, because you can cook really delicious dishes and then freeze portions so you have lots of ready-to-eat meals in the freezer that are your own specialties.

Vacations

There are lots of ways to take vacations for minimal expense. Camping, visiting friends who live in nice places, or volunteering in another country can help you get there, and afterwards, you get some precious fun time. There are websites that can connect you with places where you can do volunteer work in exchange for room and board:

HelpX offers world travelers opportunities to work on farms, ranches, homestays, and lodges. A friend of mine spent a couple months in Italy doing this, picking olives. She said that not only was she able to stay in a beautiful place and eat for free, but she got to view the area through the lens of locals and found out about all sorts of things going on that tourists traditionally never do.

There are many ways of keeping the costs down during a getaway. As I mentioned in earlier chapters, my big splurge is to take a few days by myself up the Northern California coast. Since I live with other people, I crave quiet time, where I can read and work on my writing. I love being near the ocean, and the farther north I go up the coast, the more beautiful and peaceful it is. I've found tiny cabins for rent, as well as people who rent cottages through Air BnB and then make a deal with me where I can pay them directly in the future for a lot less. I've also found websites like Priceline, Groupon, Booking.com, TripAdvisor, and others that have hotels with rooms at very low prices. And I go during off-season or on weekdays, when rates are lowest.

Friends have said they wish they could afford to do this. However, these same people prefer to spend money on takeout.. I figure the cost of a take-out sandwich and a beverage five days a week is the same as the amount I spend on my getaways. It's all a matter of trade-offs.

The California coast is nicest in the autumn or early spring. It's busiest during the summer. Thus, I plan my trips when the tourists thin out and the rates go down, but the weather is still nice. I save a lot of money by bringing my own food. Now, this is one way I am different from most people. I know that for many, eating out is part of the fun of a vacation. I pack my own food for two reasons. First is to save money. This can save a ton. The other reason is I prefer healthy choices that are often difficult to find in restaurants. I'm much happier eating what I bring with me and then going out once or twice for a treat meal. Often, I will eat lunch at a restaurant on the drive up, and then I'll eat out again on the way home. I choose places to stay that either have kitchens or at least a fridge and a microwave. Over the years, I put together a bag that contains plates, silverware, a mug, and a cutting board with a sharp knife, and I even bought plastic wine glasses. I've learned which foods can go a few days without refrigeration, like certain fruits and vegetables. Most aged cheeses can go a day or two without refrigeration.

There was a very nice hotel that had $500 rooms listed for $98 on Groupon during certain months of the year on weekdays. I had a flexible work schedule, so I took advantage of that and was able to enjoy some luxury. The only problem was that there was no fridge or microwave. I bought an electric hot pot that boiled water, so I could make tea, and I could bring instant noodle soups and add vegetables and other things, and with a bit of ingenuity, I put some pretty good meals together. I found other places that had a small refrigerator but no microwave, so eventually I bought a small, inexpensive microwave and a suitcase that it fit in perfectly, and then I had a perfect solution. I could cook delicious meals the week before my trip and bring the leftovers to store in the fridge and heat up in the microwave. When I told people about this, they'd look at me astounded. But for me, it was just perfecting my plan of living well on a shoestring. As the years passed, I added more accessories to my travel kit and experimented with different meals I could throw together. It's fun and very satisfying.

Retirement

This is one of the most overlooked areas in finance. Not only do people want to avoid thinking about what they're spending and fail to put money in a savings account for treats, but they really don't want to think about putting money away they won't be using for twenty, thirty, or forty years. This type of saving absolutely should be taught in school, but it isn't. If you have a conventional job, there is usually some form of retirement plan built into your benefit package. Either you have a pension or a 401(k), and you can have some control over how much goes in there. Many companies who offer this have a program to match some of the funds you put in. Absolutely take advantage of this if it is offered. Put in as much as you can. In a company-sponsored plan, they usually have people who take care of the investments for you, but often, you can take control if you want to. Either way, letting wealth build over decades is the way to go; $10,000 can turn into $100,000 if you start early enough. The stock market goes up and down, but it always moves higher, even if it has a few years of slump. Unless you have been tracking the market very intently, I wouldn't recommend trying to do anything too tricky to make a short-term gain. You're investing for the long haul. Putting your money in the S&P 500 is a very safe bet. This is a fund composed of the 500 best-performing companies' stocks, and it's very stable. Once you put money in there you don't have to think about it ever. Just keep a regular amount going in.

If you are worried about the risk, one thing you can do is have most of your money in the S&P 500 and then have a small amount in a money market or cash. As you get closer to retirement, this is more critical. By the time you retire, it is wise to have four to five years' worth of withdrawals in a cash-like fund so you can ride the waves of the market's ups and downs.

If you don't work for a company that has a retirement plan, open your own IRA at one of the major brokerages. There are traditional IRAs and Roth IRAs. The difference is, the traditional IRA is funded with pretax dollars, and you can deduct that amount you contribute from your taxes and get a good return from the IRS. A Roth IRA is funded with after-tax dollars. You forgo deductions on your taxes, but then, when you retire and start taking money out, it's tax free, whereas traditional IRAs are taxed when you withdraw from them, so if you go that route, you have to figure the cost of taxes into your retirement budget. One gives you a break while you are investing, and the other gives you a break once you're retired. You'll want to ask your tax person about your particular situation and what the best thing to do is. However, when you're done working and just want to enjoy your golden years, it's nice to have money you can withdraw without owing any taxes. Your 401k at work is usually funded with pretax dollars, so it will be taxed during retirement. But you can legally open your own Roth IRA in addition to having a retirement plan at work. So you can have two retirement accounts building. Few people do this. But it is a wise thing to do if you are able.

Even putting away $50 a month will grow big with compound interest over decades. I spent much of my working life self-employed, and I frequently didn't earn a lot of money as a massage therapist. Many of my clients were business owners, and they talked to me about money and investing. Those conversations convinced me to open up my own retirement accounts when I was in my thirties. The minimum amount required was $50, so many months, that was all I put in. When I could afford to, I put in more. With a Roth IRA, you need to make contributions for five years, and then you can pull money out at any time without owing taxes, regardless of your age. If you pull it out before the five-year mark, you have to pay taxes on the growth. Sometimes, a crisis hits, and you need money, and your IRA is all you have.

I implore you to take this seriously, and if you don't currently have a retirement account, open one immediately. I can't emphasize this enough. By the time you are in your sixties, it is too late to save enough to retire. You can't count on Social Security to cover everything. It has not kept up with the cost of living, so it doesn't usually cover everything most people need. That's a program the government controls, and the government is always changing. Social Security's viability gets brought up during almost every election cycle, and it's a very scary threat to millions of Americans. You definitely want to supplement it with something you have some control over. Please, please, please take this seriously. Your older self will thank you.

Self-Control Is Power

If you work at ways to keep your costs down, tucking away enough to cover emergencies and occasionally splurge on pleasure, you will feel abundant. There are a lot of clever ways to do this and come out ahead.

This is key to truly taking good care of yourself.

I like to look at this as a form of creativity. How can I eat really well without spending a whole lot of money? How can I orchestrate fabulous getaways? What's going on this week in the community that's fun and free? All of these strategies are a fun win. They are ways to have a good life while keeping you safe and secure. It's fun to watch that savings balance grow. It's exciting to know you can afford a splurge this week. What will it be? You'll be thrilled with yourself when you go on

YouTube and learn how to fix something without having to call an expensive repair person. I have a friend who built a granny unit in his backyard by watching hundreds of YouTube videos on every aspect of the project.

It's nice to be in control of your finances and know if an emergency arises, you have it covered, and if there's something you really want, you have a discretionary savings account you can tap into. This is taking care of yourself the way you would take care of someone you dearly love. Today, you are the loved one.

Exercises to Manage Finances

Create a Budget

Figure out your monthly spending and saving amounts:

- Make a list of your fixed expenses
- Make a list of other expenses, such as groceries, utility bills, gas, subscriptions, and so on
- Deduct that number from your monthly allotment
- Decide how much to put in an emergency fund
- Decide how much to put in a retirement fund
- Decide how much to put in a discretionary fund

- Decide any other allotments, such a something big you are saving up for, such as a vacation or a car or other large purchase

Create a plan for getting out of debt:

- Work on a strategy to pay off credit cards and other debts

Set goals: Where do you want to be in five years? Ten years?

CHAPTER 9

Step 6. Indulgence: Treat Yourself

Life Is Short; Buy the Shoes

This is a sign I saw in a small, independent shoe store in a local tourist town. It made me smile, because in addition to being a clever marketing slogan, it was true. We need our indulgences. They are what get us through the tough days and the tedious, boring, trying days. They help us cope, restore us, and recharge us.

We are basically human puppies, and we need our treats. Right? We crave rewards for our efforts, and who knows better how hard we are working than we do? And who knows better than us the exact delicacy that will delight us the most? Perhaps we use this reward to thank ourselves for doing something hard or something we really don't want to do, but it has to get done. Maybe we had to get up very early for a work project or to take care of something important. Or we had to confront someone about something we're dreading with nausea in the pit of our stomach. After an exhausting morning or a full day of intensity,

104

we deserve something special. It's obvious to think of a drink or going out to eat, but what are some other ways to give back to ourselves after we have poured out a ton of energy?

It could be getting a massage or a facial or going to a yoga or dance class. It could be going somewhere nearby that's a beautiful spot in the town park, a lake, or a river, and just taking some time to walk in beauty. Or going to hear some music if you live someplace that has free live concerts. In the area where I live, we have a lot of free concerts during the summer in the parks of nearby towns. Of course, it also could involve tapping the discretionary fund to buy a ticket to see a favorite musician perform.

We need soothing from something really wonderful every now and then to bring us back to that "life is good" moment. In fact, we need these spritzes of positive energy pretty darned often. Radical self-care is being your own best friend and making sure you get what you need. Indulging yourself in what will help restore you and keep you uplifted is good medicine for the soul. Sometimes, you need to take yourself out on a date. The nice thing about doing this by yourself is that you can do exactly what you want. You don't have to compromise or adjust your desires to match up with anyone else. The choice of what to do is 100 percent yours. Whenever I go to a free concert in the park in the community, I always end up dancing with people who, just like me, showed up on their own and edged toward the stage in front. There's a natural spirit of joyful community at these events. In a way, we're all there for the same reason. As we meet each other's eyes while we dance, there's an automatic smile as the music sweeps us up, and we're all enjoying that moment together while the rhythm of the band lifts us up, and we dance in sync. There's a joyful ecstasy that comes from us all connecting collectively. It's as though, on some level, we really do know each other, or at least we know as much about each other as we need to for that moment. I love events like that, when connecting with strangers is like being with people I've known forever.

Giving yourself small gifts of pleasure does not need to be expensive or fattening. It can be a candlelit bath or a drive to a beach, a park, or the woods. Sometimes, the gift is time spent doing something special, but it costs nothing. It could be attending a local art exhibit or a special event that showcases local food or something that is unique to your town.

Once you get in the habit of giving yourself special treats, you can bargain with yourself when you have to do something you really don't feel like doing, but needs to get done. Maybe you're dealing with a problem that involves a lot of miserable phone calls or paperwork. Or some grueling task you've been putting off for a while you want to get taken care of and behind you. This is a way of negotiating with yourself so you can get the job done and be well compensated for it. We'll get all the forms completed for the contract, and then we're going to the beach. Yes, it can be a bribe, and it works. It makes it easier to get hard things done when a sweet reward is waiting for you afterwards, and you know exactly the reward that makes it worthwhile.

It can also be a splurge, because sometimes, that's exactly what you need. We have a culinary school near our house, and every once in a while, I treat myself to something from their bakery. My favorite items they make are their savory pastries. Last time I went there, they had galettes made of puff pastry filled with caramelized onions, goat cheese, and butternut squash. So good! I can still remember that buttery taste and the texture of the flaky dough. Like popping into a French patisserie. Your splurge might be a piece of jewelry or a new guitar or some other treasure. Depending on what you've done, what you need, and what you like, it can vary greatly. The message here is to treat yourself well, the way you treat people you love.

The other morning, I gave myself the gift of reading in bed in my pajamas, getting up for breakfast, and then crawling back into bed for another hour of reading. It felt very indulgent. Maybe you do this all the time, but for me, it was a special treat. My day usually begins by consulting my to-do list or getting ready for my scheduled appointments. This slow morning made me feel ultra-luxurious and resulted in a more productive day.

Indulgences are a way of thanking yourself. They are a way of giving yourself love and respect and honor. This is also a way of acknowledging all the hard work you do. The great thing about this is, you are relying only on yourself, and you're the one who knows what you want and need more than anyone else does. It's highly reassuring to know you have put yourself in such wise hands.

I rarely eat out, and instead, I prefer to spend my money on road trips. These recharge me more than anything in a number of ways. I need blocks of time when I can take off and not be tethered to anything or anyone. I crave days when I can unplug from my routine and then indulge in my own world of nature, reading and writing. I figure, a month of not buying lunch or snacks covers a night at my favorite beachside cabin. We are always making choices, so make wise ones.

More than anyone else, you're the one who knows what restores you and helps you find your center again. The more you pamper yourself, the better you can be to others. My greyhound, Maggie, teaches me about this every day. A walk through the neighborhood is her treat. I try to indulge her as much as possible. It's also a time for us to bond, so that's a reward for us both. After the walk, she calms down and will curl up on her favorite cushion for a nap, no longer bouncy and overly energetic, as getting her walk puts her at peace. Maggie is one of my happiness gurus.

Taking Yourself on a Date

It's important not to put treats off to the point where we are hardly ever getting them. When we do that, our lives become a boring set of tasks we have to slog through. It can make us grumpy and give us bad attitudes. A lot of people think they need a partner to share a meal out or a few days away, or to accompany them to a movie. Many of the things I do to treat myself are activities people traditionally do with someone else: a good friend, spouse, or partner. I'm suggesting you be that partner to yourself, at least sometimes.

For some people, this may be a new concept. Sometimes, people think others will look down on them if they are doing things alone, as though they will appear lonely and sad, as if no one wants to be with them. But that's not true at all. People who enjoy their own company are some of the happiest people in the world. It gives us a sense of being complete and whole, without needing anyone else. That's a very powerful state to be in. It's actually rather enviable. The more you make time to do this, the better you will feel about yourself and your life. Think of this as giving yourself frequent joy blessings. Think of it as medicine. Think of it however you need to. I think of it as radical self-care.

I'm not big on shopping for clothes. I tend to dress pretty simply, and that probably has a lot to do with working in a field that doesn't require dressing up. My basic uniform is leggings and tee shirts, but you may enjoy buying yourself an article of clothing as a treat. A new shirt, jacket, scarf, or a new pair of shoes may be just the thing that perks you up. Indulge. Give yourself a special gift. Because life is short. Buy the shoes.

Indulgence Exercises

- Make a date on your calendar that will be time just for you.
- Make a list of your indulgences. What do you consider an indulgence?
- What do you wish you did more often? Or at all?
- Once a week, write down the indulgent things you did for yourself that week. You can even rate them, in terms of how much you enjoyed the different ways you treated yourself. This way, you learn what you really need to do to feel replenished.

CHAPTER 10

Step 7. Creativity: Letting Yourself Sparkle

What do you love to do so much that once you get started, the hours zip by, and you hardly notice? What absorbs your imagination so completely that you forget about the twenty-four-hour news cycle, your to-do list, and the fact that you really should lose ten pounds? What is that thing you get so wrapped up in that you are wondering what you can give up so you can do it more?

That is your creative passion. So, tell me. How often do you do it?

In the past six steps, I have talked about various elements, which I consider to be essential for a true recharge of your body, mind, and soul. Most of these are part of the first order of survival needs, such as rest, financial security, and nourishment. Others are important for emotional health, such as journaling, decluttering, and indulging in special pleasures.

This step is a little different. This is the one that really puts a spark into your life. This is the shine. The glitter on the forehead. The thing that makes you forget to look at the clock. Where you get so absorbed that everything else disappears.

Having a creative outlet is a very important way of channeling your energy into something that lights you up inside. When I talk about creativity, I don't mean necessarily being an artist, a writer, painter, sculptor, or craftsperson, although there are many avenues in the arts in which to pour creative energy.

I have never been able to draw well. My drawings still look like a five-year-old made them. That's not where my talent lies. And my very first semester of college was at an art school. But I still can't draw. I went there because I was fascinated with fiber and weaving, and wanted to be a fiber artist. Playing with fiber and textures and colors was something I found fascinating. I especially loved that I could make beautiful pieces out of fiber that could be clothes, scarves, handbags, and all sorts of things I could use every day. But the art school I attended did not allow anything functional. Everything we made had to be art. As far as their definition went, art could not be used for any other purpose. They considered that crafts. So I left. In my way of thinking, anything could be done as a work of art that was also functional. You see, you have to do what is in your heart. I wanted to live in a world where everything we used could be artistically designed and handmade. I dreamed of an artistic, beautiful world. I wasn't going to let a bunch of professors with degrees in art tell me that hand-designed furniture, clothes, or homes were not art. Everything can be artistic if that is the intention.

What are some things you like to make? What have you invented? It doesn't have to be anything you've sold or done as a vocation. What do you have fun making and experimenting with? Have you ever been to an art show or a crafts fair and been inspired to try something you've seen there on your own? Or been inspired to take a class the presenter is teaching? Think about some of the things you enjoy making and experimenting with.

From an early age, I started making my own clothes. It began with classes in school, where we learned the basics. I thought it was exciting to be able to go to the fabric store and choose the fabric my shirts would be made from. I liked wearing tee shirts covered with a long-sleeved shirt that came down to my mid-thigh. I couldn't find shirts this length very often in shops, so I started making my own. Once I found an easy pattern, I got an array of fabric and began making many of these shirts.

Writing has also been a creative outlet since my earliest years. It has been second nature to pour my thoughts and feelings into poetry and essays.

I love music but have never learned to play an instrument, and I cannot carry a tune to save my life. Much as I love music, it is not someplace I can pour my creative energy. I am really envious of people who have those talents because making music looks so satisfying.

We often think of creativity as applied to the arts. But there are so many other ways to express our inventiveness. Decorating your house, designing a garden, planning a party, creating a photo album, making videos, putting together music mixes. Even starting a business can be a creative endeavor.

Cooking is a great opportunity to let your experimental energy flow. Instead of using a recipe, just experiment with ingredients that sound good. If it doesn't work out, then try something else. I am always fooling around with new ideas in the kitchen. Some of the things I make are flops. But I don't mind. It's fun to play around and see what happens. I find cooking to be a very comforting, creative outlet. There's something about experimenting with recipe ideas in the kitchen I find relaxing and restorative. I am always finding leftovers or something in the fridge that needs to be used up, and I immediately start thinking about all sorts of possibilities that pop up in my mind regarding things I can do with them. It's fun. And then, it's yummy. I especially enjoy cooking in the winter. There's nothing more soothing for me on a cold, rainy day than going into the kitchen, putting on some music, and experimenting with food: making a soup, stew, or casserole or trying a new recipe I ran across.

One of the important aspects of creativity is knowing it's totally okay to screw up. Yes, that's right. Embracing the fact that some of the things we make will be failures gives us the permission to experiment. Anyone who has ever made anything they admire has had plenty of failures. That's the whole nature of experimentation. It's fun to fool around and try new things, whether they end up panning out or not. Our failures are where we learn. We learn so much from our mistakes. If you don't have a few screw-ups, it means you're not really reaching very far.

"What happens if I do this?" is one of my favorite questions. I am trying new things all the time, and many of the things I try to do don't work out. But a few of them do. And the thing is, I learn so much from experimenting and trying new things. It's really engaging.

It's always a bit disappointing to spend time cooking something that turns out unappetizing or writing something my critique group politely shakes their head at, but it just inspires me to try something else. There is no shame in trying something new, whether it ends up working out or not.

I repeat: There is no shame in trying something new.

This is the only reason anything was ever invented. Somebody got an idea and decided to try it. Some things worked out. Some didn't, but if people didn't experiment, nothing would exist.

It Doesn't Have to Make You Money

Since our culture is so strongly oriented towards accomplishment and success, we often fall into the trap of thinking if we create something valuable, we should be able to sell it. Perhaps we are talented at an art or craft, and we make beautiful paintings or something handcrafted out of wood. Friends may praise your work and tell you people definitely would buy it. That can add a whole additional way of thinking about working on a project. Once you think about selling your work, that changes the way you approach the creative process. Instead of just brainstorming and playing and experimenting, your mind naturally goes into thinking how you would display it, present it, market it to the public, and that can take away from the pure joy of just playing in the world of creative expression. Thinking about selling your work can make you afraid to take chances. That transforms pure creativity into starting a business. That's not what this is about. This is about pure play and fun. And no judgment.

I know this well, because I have done this with many things that started out as pure enjoyment. As I stated above, I like to work with fabric and sew things. I've made many of my own clothes and several years ago started making handbags exactly the way I wanted them, with compartments for all the things I carry around with me. Instead of having a large sack where I was rummaging around for my pen or my keys, I started making handbags where I sewed slots for my pens and little pockets for my keys and phone, and a built-in change purse and billfold. A friend of mine was very impressed and told me I should make them to sell at craft fairs. Cashiers also commented on how unique my handbags were. Of course, these comments went to my head. I started making handbags out of fabric I handwove on my four harness floor loom. I love weaving and find it fascinating to play with different colors and textures of yarn, and I love to see what the fabric will look like when I weave them together. My handbags are very unique because they don't look like anything commercial. Thus, I was being told over and over again that I should make them to sell.

After a while, these compliments got to me, and I decided I would start making some handbags to sell. I found out about holiday craft fairs and learned how to enter them, set up a booth, and spent many years making handbags as well as handwoven scarves and other items to sell at the fairs. I don't regret it, because I learned a lot, and it was a lot of fun to share my work. But it did take away from pure creativity. I had to make enough pieces to fill up a booth. I couldn't just show up with three handbags. So I started mass-producing items, with slight variations to make each one a little unique, but that interfered with the process of pure exploration.

I learned a lot about the life of a professional craftsperson. And yes, I learned how difficult it is to make money with one's art. A lot of time goes into the presentation, setting up for a show, being at the event while people stroll through examining everything. Afterwards, it takes a lot of time to pack up. I had professional photographers take pictures of my best pieces to use for promotional materials and developed a mailing list, mailing out postcards with photos of my work to let the people on my mailing list know when craft fairs and art shows were happening. I spent time with artists and craftspeople who had been doing this for much longer than I had and learned all the details involved in presenting the work.

I sold many pieces, but really, when it all came down to it, it wasn't really providing much money after I considered how much time I spent. Considering the time it took to go to the event location, spend the day before the event setting up the booth, spending the weekend selling things and then packing up, it's practically impossible to get paid for your time. Since I was focused on making items the public wanted to buy, I stopped experimenting. Even if my ideas didn't always work, I enjoyed seeing what would happen when I tried different things, and that would often lead to new discoveries. But once I started doing craft fairs and had to make things I was certain people would buy, I stopped trying new things. I stopped doing my dream and got sucked into the great American dilemma of trying to make my art financially successful.

Elizabeth Gilbert talks about this in her book on creativity, *Big Magic*. She cautions people about putting the burden on their creativity to support them financially.

You see, there's a big difference between diving into a medium and having fun with the freedom to invent anything, and trying to turn your work into a profitable business. Selling your art is a lot of pressure. It can transform something that was pure joy into another job. More work. More responsibility. More worries about success, about what others think, about measuring up.

Now, there's nothing wrong with turning a profit on your art. It can be very exciting to sell your painting or your published book. That can be enormously rewarding.

But it's not self-care. Once you put yourself in a position where others are judging you, a slew of unpleasant emotions come up.

Creativity for Pure Pleasure

The reason channeling your creativity is such an important part of self-care is, it makes you feel alive. Creativity is the juice of the universe.

Think of something you've made that you were very proud of. Remember how, when you were figuring it all out, your entire focus was on that moment? While you were working on your project, it became your whole world for a while. Time stopped. Or it flew by. When you are caught up in a creative project, time does not even exist. Only putting your ideas into productivity matters.

There is a kind of magic that happens when you are entirely absorbed, working on a creative project, whether you are writing a book, putting in a garden, or making art. The absorption involved in seeing how your ideas manifest in reality is very exciting. It makes you sparkle, and there is a great sense of accomplishment when you are done.

Another reason this is an important part of self-care is, you don't need anybody else to make this happen. The point of these self-care steps is, they are all things that are easily within your power. They are all ways to make your life better. Nobody else is necessary in order for you to do any of these things. When you decide to repaint your kitchen, or put in an herb garden, or whip up something new to use the leftovers in the fridge, it is your own personal inspired moment.

Just go for it. Incorporate more creativity into your life.

Exercises to Inspire Creativity

Where do you spend your creative energy? What do you like to do?

Do you have a creative project that has been incubating in your mind? Is there something you've been thinking about but haven't gotten around to starting?

- start by writing down the details
- make a list of steps involved in starting, working on, and completing the project
- set aside some time on your calendar to do the first step

Get some books on creativity. It can help a great deal to get another person's perspective. Most creative people struggle with procrastination, and getting ideas from other creative people can be very helpful.

Once you know what you want to do, decide how that will fit into your schedule, and set aside the time in order to do it.

CHAPTER 11

Step 8. Decluttering: Making Room

Get Rid of What You Don't Want to Make Room for What You Do Want

When was the last time you cleaned out a drawer, a closet, your garage, or your filing cabinet? Is this something you frequently put off for another time? Do you have piles of books, mail, papers stacked up, taking up space on tables, ledges, counters, making your home seem messy? Do you have a voice inside promising you will take care of sorting through everything? Do you fail to hold that voice accountable?

Yes, I know the feeling.

It is way too easy for us to accumulate stuff. And yes, it can be incredibly tedious and boring to pour through it and discard things that are no longer necessary. But boy, it can make such a difference. And wow, does it feel good to turn a messy room into a tidy, organized space.

An excess of stuff can really weigh you down.

Excess stuff is like having clogged arteries of the soul. Having to sift through accumulated clutter to find what we're actually looking for takes up our limited time and space. It can keep you from having the environment and the life you want. Just looking at it all can make you feel lethargic and can be a drain on your energy and sense of well-being.

I understand it can be scary to let things go because we become so deeply attached to the things we acquire. Everything has memories. However, some of these things are outdated. There are things you have that you likely don't need, will never use again, and that you are done with.

Look at it this way: What if you narrowed your belongings down to just the things you really love? How would that change your life? There's a reason the book *The Life-Changing Magic of Tidying Up* by Marie Kondo became a bestseller. Marie Kondo recommends asking yourself if items bring you joy, and if they don't, let them go.

I'm not just talking about clothes you no longer wear and things from twelve years ago sitting in the garage that you don't use anymore. I'm also talking about people who bring you down or don't give you joy. I'm including things you do out of habit that don't serve a purpose anymore. Everything and everyone who no longer supports the person you are or the person you want to be is something or someone who is unnecessary, and you need to eliminate them from your life.

Decluttering is a process of creating space of all kinds. And the thing is, once you make some room in your life, you then have an opening for something new, something better. For example, if there are activities you are doing you no longer enjoy, such as being part of a group that no longer interests you, or getting together with people you no longer feel a connection with, giving those things up makes room for something more satisfying. Decluttering can be about time as well as space.

I helped a friend who was selling her house. She was moving to a much smaller place and had to get rid of a lot of stuff. She knew she couldn't do it alone. She kept getting lost in the memories various things evoked, or she felt guilty about getting rid of something that had been a gift from a dear friend. The thing was, she had a lot of dear friends. And when she added up all the birthdays, holidays, and other important occasions from her childhood all the way to the present, she had to agree it was ridiculous to assume she could hang onto everything that had ever meant something to her. She certainly had tried, and having property with room for storage sheds and an attic definitely enabled her to let it pile up. But now she had to take a really good look at limiting her belongings to the few things she really loved and currently used that she'd have room for in her new place.

We made piles. There was a pile of things to throw away, a pile of items to donate, and a small pile of things to keep. There were times when it was wrenching for her to let something go, but it also became obvious how silly it was to hang on to toys she'd had when she was five years old because a beloved cousin gave them to her. It helped that we would donate these items to places where they could do a lot more good than clogging up her storage bins. And it felt so good to finally have some nice, clean space and order.

Filling Your Time as Carefully as Your Bookshelf

As you consider making space in your closets, you may want to do the same thing in your calendar. In an earlier chapter, we talked about the importance of time, how valuable every moment is. This is an area that can greatly benefit from decluttering. I love big blocks of unscheduled time, where I am free to go off on a day trip or on walks or even to laze around the house, seemingly doing nothing. Having time to myself helps me breathe better. It gives me much needed space. But I don't have a lot of time like that. Sometimes, I will designate one day a week, or a part of a day, just for me. I need that. I need breaks and space. We all do.

The next step here is to look deeply at your schedule and see if there's anything you're doing that you could stop doing, without it having a negative impact on anyone. Sometimes, this means asserting boundaries or declining invitations from friends or refraining from volunteering to help out. If you tend to be a helpful, giving person, it can be very difficult to stop helping others and instead make some space for yourself. But this is how we recharge, and giving ourselves a chance to soak up some much-needed alone space makes us better members of the community in the long run. It's very easy for time to fill up. Just like physical things we acquire, we volunteer for things and agree to do things that may sound good in the moment, but months or years down the road, these things can be wearing us out, and some of them are unnecessary, or they have lost their initial momentum. The trick is to let go of things that take up your time without feeling guilty.

What would you like to change about your schedule? Are there things you're doing that you want to stop? Is it hard for you to say no to people who want your attention? Look at your schedule, and see where you could carve out some more time for yourself.

I decided I needed a couple of days each week that were mine to do as I please. I needed blocks of time for writing and also for time in my garden. Both of these things are very restorative. If I didn't specifically set aside this time for myself, it got filled up. Sometimes, I had to decline invitations with friends and organize my chores in such a way that I fit everything into the time that was left, so I could have some free, open days just for me. It wasn't easy. It nags at my heart to tell a friend I can't get together this week, but if I don't have some time to myself, I start to go crazy, and I'm not a fun person to be around. So once I put myself on my schedule, I became protective of that time.

It definitely feels weird to say, "I'm sorry, but I'm busy then," when I'm really just the opposite of busy. But the truth is, busy or not, the schedule is full. It can be so hard to prioritize ourselves. A slew of emotions can come up. Guilt, certainly. But also regret. If there's someone you haven't seen in a while, it can tug at your heart to decline to get together. But sometimes, it's better to schedule a date for a time further in the future and keep the space for yourself, if that's really what you need. It definitely is possible to have room for everything you want, including yourself.

Fresh Starts

When you move to a new residence, that's an opportunity to do a lot of decluttering. After all, anything that doesn't get packed up and moved to the new place doesn't require moving boxes and have to be organized. Moving is a fabulous time to inventory your belongings and decide what you want to take with you and what you can let go. Just as my friend who was moving did, you can find great places to donate things, so that by doing this, you are helping other people. When you free yourself of the unnecessary clutter, you can begin with new priorities. This enables you to have a fresh start and not only decide what items to keep, but how you want to organize, display, and categorize things.

I've lived in the same house for over thirty years. This requires that I make a point of going through things every so often. That's when I might rummage through my garage, my attic, or my closets and see what is useful, what I can give away, and what I can toss.

Let There Be a Void

I love the sense of space that comes from a cleaned-out area, after going through the rummaging, tossing, and internal dialogue about why I keep hanging on to something. Once things are placed in a shopping bag or boxes, or even better, brought out to the car, to be taken to the thrift store, I love being able to clean the area and rearrange the few things that are left. It's not just physical space. An emotional weight is lifted. I often find I like my home so much better after I've done this.

This is the truly magical part of letting things go. When you have empty space in your home, or blocks of unscheduled time, first of all, just enjoy the peace and the tranquility that comes from making room, because that in itself is a pretty rare thing. Beyond that, you now have space for something new and wonderful to come into your life. Or you are able to enjoy the peace that comes with just a few favorite belongings or the time to relax and enjoy yourself without any pressure to do anything.

Try it. Clear something out. Make some room. And then see what happens.

Exercises for Decluttering

Choose an area of your home or workspace you want to declutter.

- Get some containers, and as you go through your things, pull out the things you can let go of and put them in the containers to be discarded, whether it's thrown away, donated, or sold.
- Make a plan for when you're going to declutter a specific area.
- Think about how you want the end result to be. For instance, if you're cleaning out your garage, what do you want your garage to ultimately look like? Keeping the vision on the end result helps you stay on track.

Make a list of people and activities that take up your time and energy but you don't enjoy. Which things can you stop doing? What people can you back off from? You don't need to have a formal breakup or make a big deal about it, but notice whom you'd like to spend less time with. Don't feel obligated to do things you don't really want to do unless you have to or if that will lead to something you want.

CHAPTER 12

Step 9. Authenticity: Be Yourself

> Be yourself. Everyone else is already taken.
>
> – Oscar Wilde

Our world is like a department store in terms of all the life paths and opportunities that are available to us. There are so many different aisles we can walk down, we hardly know which way to turn. So how do we decide?

What kind of work will suit us best?

What should we major in at college?

Should we marry or just live together?

Have children or not?

Where would be a great place to live?

Which people are the ones we want to foster friendships with?

Any decision we make comes with an array of pros and cons, so we have to be clear about what is right for us.

One of the hardest things we face can be making the choice to be different. By this, I mean following a path that radically diverges from the one that is expected of us. Living as closely as possible to this ideal is honoring your truest self, an important practice of radical self-care. The more you live in accordance with your own truth, the more you will see your life transform. You will naturally attract people and opportunities that fit the path you choose, once you commit to it. At the very least, you will feel comfortable in your own skin.

Here's an example of something that illustrates my point, although it's not life changing. I love to dance. All my life, music and rhythms have inspired me to move, and when I hear music, I can't sit still. I have to bounce up and get lost in the rhythms. On a Zen level, when I am dancing, I am 100 percent in the present. In that respect, dancing could be considered a spiritual practice of mine. It is also a form of exercise as well as a favorite way to have a good time. However, the majority of the people in my life are not big fans of dancing. My husband will dance with me if we're at an event, but he does it as way of connecting with me, not because he is moved by the music the way I am. Many of my friends are not big fans of dancing, so that's not something we do together. I often get up and dance by myself, and although no one criticizes me for it, I feel like the odd duck in my circle of friends. I finally realized I needed to get to know more people who love to dance as much as I do. It may seem like a small thing, but it's a critical part of my joy, and I want people in my life I can share it with.

There are many ways that being authentic play out. From our choices regarding how we identify with gender, religion, or spirituality, it is critical that we are honest with ourselves about what really feels like us. Often, we grow up thinking we know who we are, and we know what goals we're working towards, and then we realize at some point that this doesn't really match our true self. We may find ourselves oddly unhappy, without understanding why.

It's okay to experiment. Sometimes, we have to try many things before we find the path that feels right. For instance, we might go to school and get a degree in something and then decide after a great deal of work that it's not the right career for us after all.

I once had a doctor friend who referred many of her patients to me for massage. She told me she was looking for another doctor to share her office. A month later, she said she found someone she really liked, but they hit an impasse. Just when the lease was about to be signed, this doctor told my friend she had changed her mind. She was leaving medicine to study with her spiritual teacher.

I was quite surprised. I thought to myself, *Wow, you can do that?* When I considered the time and expense of going to medical school to become a doctor, giving that up, even temporarily, seemed like an awfully big decision. It also sounded incredibly brave for someone to change her course because of a deep longing for something else. To choose self-discovery rather than a safe, solid career was an act of pure courage. It made me curious. What does it take to be that confident? This left a strong impression on me about the importance of making the most soul-satisfying decision.

I have been studying self-development for a long time. As a massage therapist and hypnotherapist, I am in the relaxation business. Understanding what makes people feel good (or not) has been of special interest to me.

The Twisty, Bumpy Road to Self-Discovery

This same friend told me if I became a psychotherapist, she would fill my practice. She said she was looking for good therapists she could refer patients to. She even told me which school she thought I should attend to obtain my master's. I followed her advice and enrolled in a Transpersonal Psychology MA program at John F. Kennedy University in Orinda, California.

Two years into the program, I found myself at a crossroads. An opportunity presented itself that I couldn't pass up. A shopping center had been built next to a new hotel in town, and I was invited to be one of the first tenants to expand my massage business into a day spa. For a long time, my dream had been to create a healing arts center with other professionals who interfaced with the community. This gave me the opportunity to do this. I could bring together other bodyworkers where we could work as a team and create an inviting, neighborhood facility, featuring different kinds of healers. It was an outlet for my creativity, where I could bring to life a culmination of my business fantasies of having a warm, friendly, fun work environment that benefited the community as well as the people who worked there. However, getting this off the ground demanded all of my time and attention. It was impossible for me to continue graduate school at the same time.

Shortly after opening the healing arts center, I dropped out of the MA program. I made a very similar choice as that aforementioned doctor. I suspended my education, where I had spent a lot of time and incurred considerable debt, to pursue a different career path for which I had great passion. The circumstances to do this made sense, even though it was a difficult decision, and one many people might not understand.

Looking Back on Life Choices

Sometimes, when I'm faced with a tough choice, I imagine myself lying on my deathbed, looking back on my life, and I ask myself, "What do I wish I had done? What memories do I want to have right now?" It's an interesting exercise. Picturing this takes me away from the immediate situation, including the expectations of my peers, my family, and our cultural paradigm. Instead, I ask myself, what do I want to see when I look back on my life? What memories would make my soul feel satisfied?

What would you like to see when you're at the end of your life, and you're looking back on it? What do you want your memories to be?

Imagining looking back on your life in that moment, looking at the life you wish you had lived, really helps get things into perspective. It can help you make hard decisions.

There are many expectations and pressures about what we ought to do as we go through life, from teachers, our family, and even friends who see us in a certain way; we are encouraged to follow the direction they think makes sense. This may or may not fit in with who we really are. In the face of this, it can be extremely challenging to even know what our hearts want. It depends on how attached we are to pleasing other people and having their approval. What would you do if there was no one to judge you? It can be scary to consider a path that would greatly diverge from what others consider the right thing. We are constantly on the receiving end of the opinions of others. But the bottom line is that this is our life, not theirs.

And it is this very way of thinking that honors your most authentic self. Sometimes, this can be the beginning of your most important life journey.

Authentic choices don't only involve major life decisions. They come into play every day, in both small and large ways. What we decide to eat, what we wear, where we shop, how we spend our day off are all opportunities to listen to the deep longing within. What makes your whole being say yes?

Making Dreams Come to Life

When I opened my massage center, I wanted a place where people could walk in the door and find friendly people who could help them relax and let down their hair. I also loved providing a positive work environment for my staff. We had monthly meetings that began with group meditation and ended with affirmations for personal and group goals. Whenever one of my therapists had a birthday, we all went out to dinner to celebrate. Every year, I had them and their loved ones over to my house for the holidays, where I cooked up a big feast, and we sat around sharing stories, gifts, and gratitude. We were family.

This was my dream. I learned so much about how to incorporate my values into a business environment. It wasn't always easy. I had to develop leadership skills. I had to learn how to mediate between people who had disagreements. I needed to motivate people. I was making this all up as I went along, learning by trial and error. I made lots of mistakes. I watched experiments fail, and I tried new things.

It was wrenching to quit the MA program in transpersonal psychology to focus on the day spa. I loved my professors. I was deeply drawn by what I was learning about psychology. I very much wanted to be able to incorporate psychotherapy into my bodywork practice. But I had to make a choice. I knew ensuring the business's success was number one.

Here is another example. Gerald and his wife decided not to have children because they wanted the freedom to take chances with their careers. Gerald, a computer programmer, said if he had kids, he would need to make sure he had a secure job, so he would opt for positions at established companies. But he was much more excited by some of the innovative technology start-ups. Without the responsibility of having dependents to provide for, he could take a chance working for a company that might fail, knowing he would eventually be okay. With a child, such a choice would be too risky. For Gerald, having a career he loved was much more important than having a family, and his wife felt the same way.

Lots of people start businesses to follow their dreams, even when their prospects are shaky. Sometimes they succeed, and sometimes they don't. The critical thing is, they took the chance. They gave it a try. When we feel passionately about something, it's important to give that desire an opportunity to thrive. If we don't, we will always wonder what might have been. Even when endeavors don't succeed, we learn an enormous amount from the process of trying. Sometimes, the things we learn or parts of the process lead us to something else that then follows the initial endeavor. It's all part of a journey. That's the best way to look at it, as it can be hard to measure success.

Those with talent in the arts might choose simple, uncomplicated jobs that allow them time and energy to work on their creative projects, even if that means a certain amount of financial instability. As I stated earlier, it's all about trade-offs. We have to evaluate what's really and truly important and meaningful to us, and then we can figure everything else out. We need to listen to our hearts, honor our curiosity, and give space to the things we've spent years imagining and visualizing. There are some ideas that we really won't know if they're viable or not until we try them. And putting something new out into the world depends a lot on occurring at the right time as to whether or not it will be successful. So there are many factors, and it's important not to give up on your dreams.

These are some examples of career choices that may not be understood or applauded by peers who don't share the same desires. When you have a passion for something, but you don't explore it, you can spend your whole life wondering what might have been. This can eat away at you, causing deep despair. Being true to yourself with your life choices is profound self-care for your soul.

Honoring Your Uniqueness

Consider the common scenario of getting together with family for the holidays. There are usually some family members you are happy to see, some you are nervous about seeing, and possibly some who drive you crazy. These are times when you have to make some compromises in order for everyone to get along. It's also a time when you can feel the sharp difference between how you behave with the group and the freedom you have with your friends or when you're alone. Times like holiday gatherings can highlight how much you have changed from the person you were brought up to be. Once you get out into the world and have a chance to explore some of the possibilities out there, you might discover parts of yourself that never had a voice when you were growing up.

Denying yourself the chance to express yourself in your own unique way can make you feel sick inside. This happens to varying degrees with any decision where you are compromising yourself. Sometimes, deep desires are stuffed down because others would find them too different, think they're too radical, or wouldn't understand. Not being understood is sometimes the price you pay for following your heart. However, if you are married, have children, or work with people who are depending on you, it's important to take them into consideration. This may require putting things on hold or not being able to follow everything that excites you. That is the price you pay for having a life with others.

Sometimes, your self-care has to happen in smaller ways, so as not to have a negative impact on the people in your life. Therefore, as long as your decision isn't hurting anybody else, you are free to explore it. The important thing is, you know why you are making these choices, and you are choosing something that fulfills you. You know what feels right. Eventually, you will find the place where you fit. It might take a while for this to happen, so in the beginning, you have to trust your gut.

Following a life you are passionate about is a reward in itself. Allowing yourself to make room for the things and people who excite your curiosity makes you feel whole and complete. And this not only transforms your energy, but it changes the entire way you experience your life.

Exercises for Authenticity

This can be something you write about in your journal, or at least begin by thinking about something that is a critical part of who you are and what defines you, but that you need to encourage more. What does your soul crave that you are not doing?

Was there a time in your life when you were more authentic than you are now?

- What changed?
- What can you do to bring that back?
- Is there anything you deeply want to do but don't have people in your life who would understand or support it?

Do you need to get to know some new people or take a class?

- Go to an event by yourself to find some like-minded people who understand this part of you.
- What do you dream of doing, but have never done?
- What is your fantasy for the kind of life you really want?
- What holds you back from acting on your fantasy/dream/ ideal life?

Give yourself permission to be your most authentic self.

CHAPTER 13

Step 10. Balance between Giving and Receiving

One of the most important things regarding self-care is finding the balance between making an effort and recharging. There is so much for us to do all the time, it's easy to put off the things that will help us refuel because we can dismiss those things as unnecessary. We might put off taking care of ourselves until tomorrow or the weekend, but when we do that, the stress and exhaustion continue to build. And that hot bath we promised ourselves might not happen for a long time.

We need to start treating ourselves the way we treat someone we deeply care for. When I speak of balance, it's an acknowledgment that a full life includes many things. Because of our different personality types and different needs, this will vary from person to person. I encourage you to look at your life and how each day, each week is structured, to see where you might make changes to put things in better balance. How often do you find yourself thinking something you're doing is too much? What can you do to slow down? Take a break? Sometimes, just stopping and giving yourself some quiet time will help you redirect your attention.

Having good boundaries also promotes balance. When you get known as someone who can be called upon to help or to go the extra mile, people will ask for your time when they need help. It feels nice to be needed, right up until it becomes too much. And for many of us who are givers, saying we're too busy or not available can be almost impossible. But that is exactly a skill we need to develop. People will take advantage of you, if you let them. Honestly, if you don't speak up for yourself, people will have no idea they are asking too much from you. Finding ways to let people know there is a limit to what they can expect from you will serve you well, and it will be good for your relationships. Sometimes, this means you have to stop responding to someone if they don't take the hint that you can't do anymore right now. Your silence will give them the message if you are unable to state it directly. Especially if you have told them you can't do anymore, and they are still asking, or if you have a difficult time saying no, your silence will sometimes say more than words can.

It's essential to find the balance between giving and receiving. Helping others feels good. Giving not only makes the other person feel good, it makes your own heart feel good. When you see something you've done has helped someone or made a positive difference in their life, you realize how valuable your efforts are. And we are all hungry for validation. That's why we keep doing it.

I enjoy promoting the practice of kindness and helping others. Whether it's helping someone get something done or doing something that lifts a person's spirits, spreading helpfulness is one of the most powerful spiritual practices we can have.

On one of my trips out of town, I was overcome with the feeling that helping others is what life's all about. In big ways. In small ways. Offering to give a hand to a friend you know is struggling. Tipping the person who prepares your coffee. Helping a confused person find their way. Being friendly to strangers when you're out running your errands. Being helpful whenever you can. Meeting a person's eye and smiling. Or just holding their gaze for a moment so they know they have been seen. There are a thousand ways, big and small, to help people.

I went to Portland for a writing retreat, and every place I went, I encountered helpful, friendly people who made me feel good to be alive and happy about humanity. I met many strangers who were extremely kind to me and helped me with directions, because I'm terrible at finding my way in new places. I'm famous among my friends for getting lost or taking the wrong turn. They took the time to explain to me where things were and how the city was laid out, so I could understand how to find the address I was looking for.

The women at the writing workshop shared their fears and vulnerabilities in words and tears and exquisite pieces of writing that made me feel less alone and not so different. I went to this writing retreat, hoping to become a better writer, but really, what it did was open my heart. I saw so many ways people were doing what they could to help other people. The presenters gave us all books from writers they knew, whom they were supporting by sharing their books. They said they take a percentage of what they bring in from the retreat to help upcoming writers.

At the hostel-like hotel where I was staying, the staff were very friendly. They greeted me with smiles every time I entered the lobby/lounge/café area. They had a little take-out bar where they made healthy breakfasts and lunches, and they remembered each day that I wanted yogurt with their homemade granola and a fresh orange for breakfast.

The people at the front desk were patient in explaining to me how to find places in town and how to get where I was going. And in order to get a good night's sleep, they gave me a quiet room on a top floor, away from the street noise.

I was so overcome by the openness and friendliness of the people I met in this city, where I arrived alone, discovering the fresh, artistic nature of Portland. My heart was blasted open.

On the flight home, as I reflected on my four-day excursion, I thought about how delightful it was to go to a place where the people were so forthcoming and inviting. Life is all about helping each other and being good to one another, I decided.

But then I had another thought: Being an open, giving person is all very well, but we need to take care of ourselves too. One of the reasons I had such a good time that weekend is because I had so many opportunities to be on the receiving end for a change, instead of always being the one extending myself.

One of the reasons we are here (or if I want to get all pompous about it, one of the meanings of life) is to find the balance between helping others and taking care of ourselves. When people go too far to the extreme in either direction, devastating things can happen.

When taking care of oneself obliterates everything else, it turns to greed, which can become arrogance or even war, at the most extreme level. And giving too much of oneself, without taking time to recharge, can result in a state of severe depletion, or becoming addicted to being needed, at its worst. We can get stuck craving the validation that comes from being appreciated every time we offer help.

Finding that balance between helping others and helping ourselves is a tricky dance. Like any balancing act, it is easy to tip to one side or the other. It feels so good to do something for someone else, where you can immediately see your action is making a difference. It also feels good to unplug, slow down, and indulge in something rejuvenating. When tackling anything big, the best thing to do is, take small bites. Go back forth. Find the comfort zone between manageable acts of giving and bite-sized treats of self-care.

It's important to look at our schedules and see how much time we are spending working and expending energy outwardly;

we need to balance that with personal time doing things that revitalize us. This includes how much time we spend socializing, versus being alone, how much time we spend reading the news and time getting lost in a novel. If you are someone who needs quiet time to recharge, make sure you are scheduling it. Set aside a day or part of a day just for you and what you need. Some people need a lot more alone time than others, so rather than copy someone you admire, check in with yourself, and listen to what your soul is crying out for. If we all did this automatically, books like this would be unnecessary. We need reminders, and we need this behavior modeled for us. We need to remember that taking care of ourselves is essential to having the strength and resilience to do everything else we want to do.

Exercises to Manage Balance

- How is your life out of balance?
- What takes up too much of your energy? What do you need to do less of?
- What helps you feel recharged? How often do you do that? How can you restructure your life so you can do that more?
- What do you need more of in your life?
- Make a commitment to yourself to reorganize how you spend your time so you can feel more balanced.

CHAPTER 14

Making Your Way through the Chaos

Although technology is a great thing, making tasks that once took forever nearly instantaneous, it is not without its drawbacks. One of the biggest problems I see is, since so much information is available to us through computers and mobile devices, we are swimming in an ocean of information. Seriously, it is a huge wave that crests over us at all times, and just like a real wave that rises up as we're barefoot in the sand, standing in the shallow water, watching it coming for us, we can easily lose our balance and get knocked over.

Between articles to read from every publication imaginable, to continuous social media posts, texts from friends and colleagues needing our attention, emails and other private messages, it's amazing we ever have a spare moment for ourselves. I didn't even mention phone calls, which are becoming increasingly rare, although there was a time when phone calls were the only disruption we had.

Develop Boundaries

Even though it's possible to walk away from technology for periods of time, checking to see the latest tweet, post, or message has become a powerful habit for most of us. It's hard to refrain from checking in and getting lost. I can't tell you the number of times I have picked up my phone in order to add something to my shopping list or check the weather app, only to fall down the rabbit hole, becoming distracted by a text or private message that then leads to other distractions, and I forget why I picked up the phone in the first place.

This continuous wave after wave of content that seduces our attention does not leave us much time for ourselves. In fact, when we take breaks, we often wonder if we are missing something. It's very hard to step away for very long. And so, we become rattled as our focus becomes split into tiny slivers, paying attention to as many things as possible, frequently multitasking and becoming overwhelmed.

Somewhere in there, we get lost. We lose control of our time. We lose our focus. Our lives become a dance where we are pulled in multiple directions, often simultaneously, doing everything we can to keep up. We go through the day, getting things done in between moments of constantly checking in. When a task is completed, we quickly grab our phones to see what we've missed. Or we even take a look during the process of getting something done. It goes on like this from the moment we wake up until we go to sleep. There is always something new to pay attention to, twenty-four hours a day.

This is how stress takes over and why we never have time for the things that really nourish us.

In order to put these self-care activities into practice, we have to begin to develop strong boundaries. Being at the beck and call of everyone else becomes a habit, whether it was intentional or not. We get used to certain life rhythms, certain patterns of behavior that eventually become what's normal for us.

In order to use these steps I have laid out, begin by choosing something you want to change in your life habits. Then, figure out how and when you're going to do it. For instance, if you need some quiet time for yourself, make a decision about when that's going to be, and then refuse any other offers that threaten to eat it up. If you need time to write in your journal, decide when you're going to do that. Perhaps after you leave work, you decide to go to a café and spend half an hour sitting in the corner, enjoying a delicious beverage and a snack and writing. After that, you go home and have dinner and continue your regular evening routine. If that protocol after work is effective, plan to do that a few days a week, and soon that will become part of your normal pattern.

A huge part of self-care is saying no to things that are going to get in your way. In fact, if this is going to work, you have to get comfortable saying no a lot. If you are someone who is used to accommodating other people, it will be difficult to say you're sorry, you're going to be busy, you can't do it. It may even be emotionally wrenching to refuse to help someone in favor of doing something your spirit desperately needs. You need to make yourself a priority.

Here's a game you can play with requests from others. In your mind, assign a color to each person's request. Red can be an emergency that really does need your immediate attention. Orange can be assigned when someone thinks they need you more than they really do. In other words, they would like your help, but they can manage without you if you're unavailable. Yellow is neutral. You have been invited to something. People would like you to come. But if you don't, life will go on just fine. Green is an offer to do something you'd enjoy but will take you away from what you've already got planned, so you can take a raincheck. Blue is something you don't want to do and you don't have to do, but in the past, you would have agreed in order to be polite. And so on. Assign colors to things that come up that get in the way of you taking time for yourself. Or in the case of budgeting, things you really don't need to spend money on so you can set it aside for things you really want.

This color assignment game helps you become aware of how important things really are or aren't that keep you from doing things for your own sense of well-being. It breaks through your unconscious behavior that has had your head spinning, not knowing where your time or money went. Once you become aware of things that pull you away from your plan, you can recognize them and start to develop a series of responses to protect yourself from getting pulled away. These are the new habits you are creating. Telling people, "Thanks, but I can't right now," or "I'm in the middle of something, but I'll get back to you in a few days," start to become your new protocols. Have a few stock phrases, so you don't have to think about what you're going to say. After a while, the people in your life will get used to the fact that you aren't going to drop what you're doing to accommodate them the way you once did. People respond to the cues you send out. They know who they can reach out to and who they should leave alone. Eventually, the people in your life will learn to respect you, when you make it clear you need space.

You need to limit the amount of time you spend checking in with technology. I have been making a practice of avoiding technology at the beginning and end of the day, so my mind is not bombarded when I need to calm down to go to sleep or when I need to feel refreshed when I wake up. I usually check email only once a day. Since I don't use email for work, I can get away with this.

CHAPTER 15

The Greatest Gift You Can Give Yourself

Once you get into a rhythm of incorporating things to take care of yourself, you start to experience life differently. You will find you are more independent and more in control of your own happiness. When you need to feel better, you know what to do. This is powerful, and it feels great.

The gift you are receiving through this new way of living is a sense of autonomy. Give yourself a minute to let that sink in. This means you are less dependent on the opinions and the time and attention of others in order to feel good, and more able to enjoy your life and give yourself what you need. This is a big deal.

There is no substitute for the love and care you give yourself. There is no one who is as dependable as you are as far as knowing what you need and how to get that need met. I'm not saying we don't need other people. Of course we do. But we cannot depend on them as much as we can depend on ourselves. Taking care of yourself makes you a stronger, more independent person. It is beneficial for you and for everyone else in your life.

The best way to use the practices in this book is to start with one or two changes you want to make. Being mindful of the things you do that shape your life helps you when you realize you need to make changes. Little by little, making adjustments that will give you more of what your soul is craving will transform your life profoundly. Adjusting your routines and thew way you treat yourself so you really are getting what you need and want from life is the greatest gift you can give yourself.

It gets easier over time. Just like any habit, taking better care of yourself starts to become your new way of living. Once you see how good it feels to do the things that really recharge you, it becomes easier to protect the time you need to do them. You start to have favorite places to go when you need alone time, whether it's to write in a journal, go for a walk, or disappear into a natural setting. You develop new patterns. As you notice the difference it makes to carve out time and special activities for your own well-being, you do it more often until it becomes your new normal.

Your life is your own unique work of art.

Enjoy being your own best friend.

Let this be an opportunity to release old patterns and habits that are not working for you, and try some new ways of going about your life that serve you better.

This is your chance to live how you want, do what you want, and be treated the way you want.

You are in charge.

Nothing can stop you now.

Printed in the United States
by Baker & Taylor Publisher Services